THERE IS A BETTER WAY

A NEW ECONOMIC AGENDA

John Grieve Smith

Anthem Press

THERE IS A BETTER WAY

by John Grieve Smith

ISBN 184331 021 X

Printed in the UK by Albert Gait Ltd

Anthem Press

Anthem Press is an imprint of the Wimbledon Publishing Company
P.O. Box 9779, London SW19 7QA Fax: (+44) 20 8944 0825

For my family

Contents

Preface

Although much of this book is devoted to discussion of economic policies, the underlying issues concern basic human values and political objectives. The Thatcherite revolution and the economic principles on which it was based led to fundamental changes in the nature of British society and gross increases in inequality. Whether from expediency or conviction, New Labour has now adopted similar policies, although these are basically inconsistent with the Labour Party's long-standing objective of achieving a fairer and more equal society. In criticising the neo-liberal economic consensus, or New Orthodoxy, on which these policies are based, my object is to stimulate discussion of the fundamental issues facing us today, and put forward alternative policies based on the assumption that all our citizens are of equal worth, that the unemployed or youngsters in deprived areas count for as much as highly paid financial executives or company directors. (If any of my friends feel that I am too critical of the policies now espoused by New Labour, I can only say that I was equally critical of the same policies when they were pursued by previous Conservative governments – as indeed were most of Labour's present leaders!)

Although the discussion is centred on UK experience, many of the issues involved are a common feature of current economic policies throughout the Western world. The neo-liberal economic consensus also dominates the behaviour of international economic organisations like the IMF and OECD. I am concerned to establish a new economic agenda not just for the UK, but also for the European Union and the global economy as a whole.

I should like to thank Michael Cowdy, Michael Franklin, Geoff Harcourt, Bill Keegan, Jonathan Michie and Frank Wilkinson for reading all or part of the draft manuscript and making helpful comments. They are, of course, not responsible for the final result.

I should also like to record my continuing indebtedness to Robinson College and the Robinson College Economic Research Fund for providing the facilities to enable me to pursue my work on economic policy.

Last, but by no means least, I must express my thanks to Mandy Barker for undertaking so efficiently and cheerfully the secretarial work without which the book would never have been finished.

JOHN GRIEVE SMITH

Cambridge
May 2001

Acknowledgements

The author expresses his thanks to the Fabian Society and Spokesman Books respectively for permission to use material from the pamphlets *Closing the Casino: Reform of the Global Financial System* and *Welfare Reform: Means-Tested versus Universal Benefits*.

Chapter 1

THE NEW ORTHODOXY

I do not know which makes a man more conservative – to know nothing but the present, or nothing but the past.

John Maynard Keynes

1. INTRODUCTION

Despite their day-to-day tactical infighting, New Labour and the Conservatives now share much the same basic political assumptions and economic philosophy. Instead of overturning the Thatcherite revolution of the 1980s, which initially they so bitterly opposed, New Labour spent their first term in office consolidating it, and seem set to continue the process in their second term. Many of their policies, and much of their rhetoric, now reflect what might be termed the 'Thatcherite consensus', rather than any new 'Third Way'. But whereas the previous post-war consensus, which Mrs Thatcher and her allies overthrew, was essentially left of centre and consistent with Labour's basic beliefs, the current consensus is firmly on the right of the political spectrum, and at odds with the achievement of a fairer society, which has always been a common objective among the many strands of opinion within the Labour movement. The neo-liberal economic philosophy on which it is based is in many respects a reversion to the pre-Keynesian ethos of the inter-war era, and provides no answers to the problems of today's unstable global economy – any more than it did in the 1920s and 1930s.

Under Tony Blair and Gordon Brown, New Labour's response to the election defeats of the 1980s and 1990s was a striking case of 'throwing out the baby with the bathwater'. They went to extraordinary lengths to disown their predecessors' policies – often subscribing to the most inaccurate and misleading versions of history in doing so. In power, their deference to the rich and powerful, the fact that they are so much more sensitive to the interests of finance than those of industry,

1

and their patronizing and authoritarian approach to the unemployed and others on benefit are all indications of a seismic shift to the right. One consequence is that, to find new political territory of their own, the Conservative Party under William Hague began to flirt with dangerously extreme right-wing views on issues like race, immigration and Europe; whilst many former Labour supporters, and people who would otherwise be active in the Labour Party, now feel disenfranchised. It is time to re-examine the neo-liberal economic assumptions underlying the current consensus and establish a more effective policy approach designed to ensure a better and fairer society not just in this country, but throughout the European Union and in the global economy as a whole – policies which will give us greater control over our economic destiny, and not leave us subject to the vagaries of financial markets and dominated by the ethos of financial institutions.

Full employment

The touchstone of economic policy in the post-war period has been Governments' attitudes to full employment. The maintenance of full employment is not merely about the number of people who can get jobs (important though that is), but also about the fundamental nature of society and the balance of power within it. In the post-war era when jobs were plentiful and new employees hard to get, workers, and the trade unions that represent them, were in a relatively powerful position. Governments listened to the unions. Managers had to pay attention to the views of their staff. Society was more egalitarian. The deliberate abandonment of full employment in the 1980s under Mrs Thatcher weakened the power of labour – as it was intended to do, not merely to slow down the rate of inflation, but to 'put the unions in their place'. It became fashionable to talk about 'the right to manage', rather than management by consent. Inequalities in rewards which would have been unacceptable in earlier years became the norm. State provision of social security, health and education, which were basic to the standard of living of the ordinary citizen, were regarded as less important than reducing the levels of taxation on the well-to-do. There was a revolution in society with which we are still living today.

At first the Labour Party was bitterly opposed to the new approach, but in time it came to accept the new Thatcherite orthodoxy. Neil Kinnock deliberately excluded full employment from Labour's objectives, and by the time of his Mais Lecture in 1995, Tony Blair was talking about 'a new economic consensus'. New Labour's adherence to the New Orthodoxy has not only affected their economic policies, domestic and international, but also their approach to policy over a much wider field, including regional policy, welfare reform, income distribution, transport, education and health. The new philosophy, fashionable as it may be, not only conflicts with the fundamental objectives – or what should be the fundamental objectives – of any left of centre government; but the circumstances which led to its introduction no longer exist. Inflation is no longer the main danger facing the world economy. Neo-liberal economic policies offer no solutions to the problems of maintaining stability in an international economy increasingly subject to the vagaries of global financial markets.

Despite the return of the phrase 'full employment' to their vocabulary as unemployment continued to decline, Tony Blair and Gordon Brown have not adopted the policies needed to achieve it. Instead they have embraced the New Orthodoxy even more enthusiastically than their Conservative predecessors. This was dramatically demonstrated by the way in which the new Chancellor announced the granting of independence to the Bank of England to fix interest rates within days of the 1997 election. This was later accompanied by statements that budgetary policy (i.e. changes in taxation or public expenditure) would no longer be used as an instrument of demand management. Although this might appear a purely technical matter, it is in fact one of major political significance. Taken at its face value, it means that what should be one of the major responsibilities of any democratic government, control over the level of demand for goods and services and hence the level of employment (in other words, people's jobs), had been passed over to a group of technicians – the Monetary Policy Committee. The alleged justification for this move is that politicians are too concerned with short-term electoral considerations to be trusted with such important decisions for the long-term health of the economy as monetary policy. But if this applies to monetary policy, why not to other major aspects of policy – public expenditure or defence, for example?

The underlying reason for the now fashionable view that monetary policy should not be under the control of democratic governments is the potential conflict between the objectives of keeping down inflation and maintaining a high level of employment. Central bankers tend to be much less concerned about unemployment than the politicians and hence if the threat of inflation is the overriding concern demand management is regarded as safer in their hands. This approach is reflected in the Government's remit to the Bank, which sets them an inflation target of 2½ per cent with no mention of other objectives such as a high level of output and employment, or stable and competitive exchange rates.

The implicit assumption that inflation is the overriding problem, rather than the maintenance of full employment, reflects the abandonment of the post-war Keynesian consensus by the 1979 Thatcher Government. Although ostensibly a response to the sharp rise in inflation in the 1970s, the Thatcherite revolution reflected a deep change in political values and objectives. To understand the emergence of today's consensus, it is necessary to look back at the evolution of economic policy over the whole post-war period.

2. THE EVOLUTION OF POST-WAR POLICY

The postwar consensus

Policy in the years immediately after World War II was dominated by a cross-party determination not to go back to the mass unemployment which had blighted so many lives in the inter-war years. Wartime experience had shown that full employment was possible if there was a high enough demand for labour; it made it plain that inter-war unemployment had reflected a shortage of jobs, not the unwillingness or inability of people to work. Maynard Keynes's thesis in his 1936 classic *The General Theory* that mass unemployment was due to inadequate demand for goods and services had gained widespread credence. Keynes's position in the Treasury during the war, together with the influx of like-minded economists, in particular James Meade in the Economic Section of the Cabinet Secretariat, meant that his views were a major influence in the preparation

4

of the 1944 White Paper on Employment Policy which encapsulated the coalition government's commitment to post-war full employment.

The 1944 White Paper

The White Paper recognized that in the immediate aftermath of war the problem was unlikely to be any shortage of demand, but rather 'to secure with a limited labour force an adequate production of goods needed to improve our standard of living and increase our exports'. But once the period of transition to a peacetime economy was over, they had to resolve the 'long-term problems connected with the maintenance of an adequate and steady volume of employment which eluded solution before the war'. Keynes had pinpointed fluctuations in investment as a major source of instability in total demand, and the White Paper reflected this emphasis. It accepted that 'Monetary Policy alone, however, will not be sufficient to defeat the inherent instability of capital expenditure. High interest rates are more effective in preventing excessive investment in periods of prosperity than are low interest rates in encouraging investment in periods of depression' – something of which the Government might well take note today. The answer lay in the use of public investment as 'an instrument of employment policy', not merely keeping it stable, but bringing public sector schemes forward or holding them back to offset fluctuations in private investment.

This represented a victory for Keynes and those in the Liberal and Labour Parties who had advocated investment in public works as a remedy for unemployment in the 1920s and 1930s – an idea that pre-dated Keynes's development of any formal theory of demand. Indeed as early as 1917, a policy resolution proposed by J.R. Clynes and passed at the 1917 Labour Party conference stated that:

> the Government can, if it chooses, arrange the public works, and the orders of the National Departments and Local Authorities in such a way as to maintain the aggregate demand for labour in the whole Kingdom (including that of capitalist employers) approximately at a uniform level for year to year; and it is therefore the first duty of the Government to prevent any considerable

or widespread fluctuations in the total numbers employed in times of good or bad trade.[1]

But throughout the inter-war period any proposals to combat unemployment by increasing government borrowing for public works ran up against the orthodox 'Treasury view', that to do so would only be at the expense of a similar amount of private investment. This was clearly not the case when resources were underused and bankers were prepared to make available the necessary finance.

Reflecting disagreements in the Treasury, the White Paper was exceedingly cautious about the use of changes in taxation to stimulate or damp down consumer demand. It did, however, give an airing to James Meade's scheme to vary national insurance contributions for this purpose – a proposal which had the practical merit that contributions were levied on a weekly basis and could be varied at any time during the financial year; whereas income tax was levied on an annual basis and could only be varied at Budget time.

Beveridge and full employment

In the same year as the White Paper, William Beveridge published his own report *Full Employment in a Free Society* as a sequel to the Beveridge Report on Social Insurance. Beveridge went further than the White Paper and proposed a more radical approach to the stabilization of private investment, with a National Investment Board encouraging and controlling investment. He also argued for the extension of the public sector of industry so as to bring monopolies under control and increase the scope for stabilizing investment. This was part of the case for Labour's nationalization proposals in 1945. Conversely when the reaction against the Keynesian consensus took hold, one of the arguments adduced by the right was to identify demand management to achieve full employment with the existence of a large state sector.

Controlling demand

The extent, if any, to which it is appropriate to use the various instruments of variations in interest rates, public investment, current government expenditure or taxation as means of controlling demand has been a continuing subject of discussion and controversy throughout the post-war period. But until 1997, all post-war governments relied heavily on changes in tax rates and all forms of public expenditure, even when monetarism was the official creed. Indeed, in the early post-war years no use was made of variations in interest rates. They were kept as low as possible to minimize the cost of servicing the wartime debt. The first Chancellor in the 1945 Labour government, Hugh Dalton, followed a 'cheap money policy' which resulted in bank rates remaining frozen at their 1939 level of 2 per cent until Rab Butler, the new Tory Chancellor, raised them to 2½ per cent in November 1951, and then to 4 per cent in the following March. Thereafter monetary policy became more active, but only as an adjunct to fiscal policy until the monetarist revolution in the 1980s.

In the immediate post-war years (as I know from my own experience in Whitehall in the early 1950s), the influence of the Keynesian economists in and around the Treasury was directed to using budgetary policy to curb the high level of pent-up demand and thus make possible the gradual dismantling of wartime controls and rationing. There is no substance to the myth, strangely perpetuated by New Labour, that full employment was maintained by pumping up demand and running large budget deficits. There was no need. Only in a small minority of cases did Chancellors have to introduce deliberately expansionary budgets to meet the threat of rising unemployment: Butler in 1953 and Heathcoat Amory in 1959 (both Tory Chancellors). The initial stimulus of post-war reconstruction, and confidence that full employment would be maintained ensured that the economy generated its own momentum.

Inflation in the 1970s

Beveridge foresaw the fact that the strengthened bargaining power of labour under full employment could cause inflationary problems: 'There is a real danger that sectional wage bargaining, pursued without regard to its effects upon prices, may lead to a vicious spiral of inflation, with money wages chasing prices and without any gain in real wages for the working class as a whole.' This problem was successfully tackled in the first 25 years or so after the war by a series of *ad hoc* prices and incomes policies. In what Michael Stewart has described as the 'Jekyll and Hyde years', the party in opposition routinely criticized the measures adopted by the government of the time and then found itself forced to take similar measures when it was in office.[2] But no permanent machinery to ensure that wage increases were consistent with keeping inflation in check was ever established. Nevertheless from 1946 to 1979 UK inflation averaged 3.6 per cent a year despite the 1950 commodity price boom and the Korean War, while unemployment remained below 3 per cent throughout. It was the inflationary pressure resulting from the boom in primary product prices in the early 1970s and the succeeding oil crises that set in motion the forces that led to the break-up of the post-war economic settlement.

Neither the Heath government which took office in 1970 nor the Wilson government which succeeded it in 1974 was able to reach any lasting agreement with the unions on pay policy, with the consequence that the period was characterized by dramatic industrial disputes and high inflation. Between 1970 and 1979 retail prices trebled. It is the reaction to those events that has dominated economic policy ever since, first in the measures that the 1979 Thatcher government took to break the wage/ price spiral and then in the emergence of the current consensus on economic management.

Under Harold Macmillan and Ted Heath, the Conservative Party remained committed to the post-war consensus on full employment, although there were undercurrents of discontent on the right of the party. These surfaced in what Peter Jenkins described as the 'seminal text' of the Conservative intellectual revolution, Keith Joseph's 1974 speech identifying the commitment to full employment as the error from which the whole drift to 'ungovernability' had stemmed.[3] He argued that abandoning full employment would rob public spending of its macroeconomic function and clear the way for reducing the size of the public sector. Inflation should be tackled by controlling the money supply. When the Thatcher government took office in 1979, monetarist theory provided the intellectual cover for a series of savage deflationary measures which brought unemployment to over three million, where it remained for five years and broke the inflationary cycle. Helped by the fact that commodity prices passed their peak in 1980, and oil prices in 1981, the rate of inflation fell from a peak of 22 per cent in May 1980 to 12 per cent in May 1981. Prices rose more slowly in 1982 and then increased at an average rate of 5 per cent for the rest of the decade.

Margaret Thatcher's two basic objectives of getting inflation under control and breaking the power of the unions were inextricably linked. It is significant that in her memoirs[4], she constantly reverts to the theme of conflict with the National Union of Mineworkers, but there is only one mention of the massive increase in unemployment. The idea that the over-mighty trade unions were the fundamental cause of Britain's economic problem in the 1970s was fundamental to the new brand of conservatism. What is surprising is the way it has become a part of New Labour mythology.

The worldwide outbreak of inflation put exceptional strains on the economy. The basic problem was not the unions as such, but the natural unwillingness of the working population (at all income levels) to accept pay increases below the rate of inflation and thus a reduction in their standard of living. The unions were the vehicle that expressed this reluctance on behalf of their members: they were not the basic cause of it – though it is arguable that in certain cases they could have shown greater restraint. The experience of the 1970s illustrates the *momentum effect* of inflation. Once inflation has reached a certain rate, people expect pay increases of a similar amount or more. It is thus very difficult to slow down inflation once it has got a grip. Conversely when, as at present, inflation is running at a relatively low level, it tends to remain there. The danger is that when any external 'shocks', such as the oil price crises, boost the rate of inflation, it is difficult to get it down again. The true lesson of the 1970s is that the only way to achieve this without sacrificing full employment is to have in place more effective machinery for discussing and influencing pay negotiations, not to scrap any such machinery altogether.

New Labour are very wary of taking such a direction, because they are frightened that to do so would risk getting ministers involved in politically embarrassing industrial disputes. The lesson they take from the Thatcher years is that such disputes are much more damaging

9

electorally than high levels of unemployment. After all, did not the Conservatives win the 1983 general election when unemployment had risen to 12 per cent, and then go on to win again in 1987 and 1992 with unemployment still around 10 per cent? But while the politicians fared better, the people paid a heavy price. The average number of working days lost per year through labour disputes fell from an average of 13 million in the 1970s to seven million in the 1980s. But the average number of days lost through unemployment rose from over 240 million to nearly 650 million. In other words, the amount of extra working time lost through higher unemployment was 70 times greater than that gained from a reduction in industrial disputes.

3. THE NEW ORTHODOXY

Monetarism

In its first years in office, monetarism was the official creed of the new Thatcher government. The core of the monetarist approach was that inflation was purely a monetary phenomenon. The original monetarist theory as set out by Milton Friedman[5] postulated that the rate of inflation depended on the rate of increase in the supply of money in the form of cash and bank credit. Thus if the growth of the money supply was properly controlled, so would be the rate of inflation. This assumption was, however, based on the faulty hypothesis that because the money supply tends to increase more rapidly when prices rise faster, the former is the cause of the latter. As is so often true in such cases, the causal sequence is not nearly so simple. The relationship depends to a large extent on the fact that the banking system is there to supply the credit needed to enable the economy to operate smoothly, and when prices rise, the supply of money will automatically tend to rise in response. It is true that the availability and cost of credit affect the ease with which prices and wages can be increased, but only through their effect on business conditions, not by any automatic direct link between the quantity of money and prices.

What might be called 'pure monetarism', with its emphasis on the money supply rather than interest rates, did not last very long. The proliferation of financial institutions taking deposits or giving credit, like building societies, raises problems about defining 'money'; and after struggling with a growing number of definitions of the money supply (M1, M2, M3, M4, M5 etc.) the Bank of England was forced to give up setting any specific money supply target. Instead it now targets the inflation rate directly and the emphasis is on interest rates rather than the money supply.

The most dangerously misleading part of the original monetarist thesis was that controlling the money supply would not affect unemployment, save in the short run. In their view, unemployment reflected 'imperfections' in the labour market to be tackled by such measures as legislation to curb the trade unions and by abolishing or weakening machinery to regulate wages (such as Wages Councils). Short of such structural changes there was a 'natural rate of unemployment' to which the economy would eventually revert. The Thatcher experiment illustrated that this was clearly not the case. While restricting credit and raising interest rates eased the pressure to raise prices and wages, it did so only by reducing sales and output, and hence increasing unemployment. This led to a change of emphasis, from treating the consequent unemployment as a temporary blip to regarding it as the necessary cost of keeping down inflation: 'a price well worth paying', to use Norman Lamont's famous phrase when he was Chancellor of the Exchequer – an honest and accurate summary of the philosophy underlying the current approach to macroeconomic policy.

The eagerness with which the monetarist prescription was seized on in right-wing circles had little to do with economics; it was a long-awaited excuse to demolish the Keynesian consensus with its reliance on government action and emphasis on the role of the public sector in helping to stabilize demand. To the Thatcher and Reagan generation, it provided the intellectual excuse for cutting back the role of the State, a return to free market economics, and a shift in power and income away from the trade unions and those they represent – all in the generally accepted cause of meeting the threat of inflation.

The New Orthodoxy

What is remarkable, however, is the way in which those on the centre and left of the political scene became infected by the monetarist virus. Just as the Keynesian revolution spread rapidly across the whole political spectrum to establish a new consensus, so today monetarist ideas have provided much of the basis for a new political and economic orthodoxy, with differences in emphasis, rather than fundamentals, between the leadership of major political parties. On the continent, Socialist and Social Democrat parties have become prisoners of the same basic ideology as the Christian Democrats and other right-wing parties, so that while they remain concerned about the high level of unemployment they are trapped in an intellectual framework that effectively inhibits them from doing anything useful about it. Thus a French Socialist, Jacques Delors, was responsible for setting the almost completely monetarist framework for the future of European integration in the Treaty of Maastricht.[6]

The consensus which has now emerged, the New Orthodoxy, may be summarized as follows:

1. Inflation should be controlled by the use of interest rates, preferably in the hands of an independent central bank.
2. The budget should be balanced rather than used as a means of influencing demand.
3. Unemployment should be regarded solely as a problem of the labour market.

This is in effect the doctrine now generally accepted by finance ministers and their advisers, together with most international organizations like the OECD and the European Commission. It is the basis of all New Labour's economic policies, but is fundamentally inconsistent with the maintenance of full employment.

During the full employment consensus, governments of both parties worked on the assumption that there was a *maximum* level of unemployment that was politically acceptable, and that economic policies must be operated within this constraint. By contrast the essential feature of the New Orthodoxy is the need to maintain a *minimum* level of unemployment to keep inflation in check. Such a minimum level of unemployment (known by the hideous acronym NAIRU – the 'non-accelerating inflation rate of unemployment') is fundamental to the thinking of both the Bank of England and the Treasury. Sometimes it is expressed in the politically more acceptable form of an 'output gap', i.e. the amount by which the level of output exceeds (or falls short of) the level at which inflation could accelerate; but that comes effectively to the same thing. What the jargon about NAIRU and 'output gaps' boils down to in plain English is that there must be enough unemployment to limit the bargaining power of the unions – a strange basis for a Labour government's economic policy, one might have thought, and not one to which even post-war Conservative governments would have subscribed before the Thatcher era.

4. NEW LABOUR IN POWER

Although New Labour's macro-economic policies during their first term of office have generally been regarded as largely successful – in that demand was strong and unemployment continued to decline until the spring of 2001 – this can hardly be attributed either to the Government's fiscal policies, which were not intended to influence the course of demand, or to any particular skill on the part of the Monetary Policy Committee. It is more a reflection of the expansionary forces already at work and of the generally favourable international environment, despite the Asian crisis of 1997–8. This apparent success does not, however, extend to the manufacturing industry, which has been badly hit by the over-valuation of the pound. The bias towards high interest rates (and hence a high exchange rate) inherent in the current approach of relying solely on monetary policy to regulate demand, and making the control of inflation its only objective, has exacted a heavy toll. The appreciation of sterling in the last two years of the Conservative government continued under Labour, accentuated by the weakness of the euro. This has caused serious difficulties for the motor, steel and other manufacturing industries, especially those competing closely with producers in the EMU. The real test for policy may yet be to come, if an American recession leads to a general slow-down in the world economy.

Gordon Brown's fiscal rules

In contrast to the empirical approach of Kenneth Clarke, his Conservative predecessor as Chancellor, Gordon Brown has committed himself to the pure milk of the New Orthodoxy in a striking manner. The Chancellor has not only abdicated any power over monetary policy in favour of the Bank of England, and given it a remit solely concerned with inflation. In addition, he has bound himself by a rigid set of *fiscal rules*, which in principle (though perhaps not in practice) rule out any active use of budgetary policy to curb inflation or avoid recession. The two new rules for fiscal policy are[7]:

1. The so-called *golden rule*: over the economic cycle the Government will borrow only to invest and not to fund current expenditure.
2. Public debt as a proportion of national income will be held over the economic cycle at a stable and prudent level.

A key feature of these rules is their deflationary bias. Budget deficits are ruled out, but not surpluses. Public investment must be held in check. This atavistic return to pre-war orthodoxy was presumably intended to impress financial markets – which it has done, but in so doing has driven sterling up to a level which has done serious industrial damage. As regards the golden rule, surpluses have been easy to achieve while the economy has been expanding strongly. Where the Chancellor has short-sightedly reduced his room to manoeuvre is in ostensibly ruling out any expansionary fiscal measures (i.e. tax cuts or increases in public expenditure) if the economy is threatened with recession. This could create a serious dilemma.

The rule requiring the public debt to GDP ratio to be held at a stable level is quite inappropriate in varying and unpredictable circumstances. It has also contributed to the disastrous continuation of the Public Finance Initiative and the introduction of the Public-Private Partnership (discussed in the next chapter). In his classic study *Major Recessions*, Christopher Dow writes,

> Debt levels have in fact varied greatly without noticeable effects on the performance of the economy. For instance, the UK

national debt in relation to GDP, already high before the Napoleonic War, rose to about 290 per cent by 1815, then fell continuously to about 30 per cent by 1914. World War I took it back to 200 per cent; in the inter-war period it fell back only moderately (to 150 per cent); then World War II again nearly doubled the ratio, taking it back to over 270 per cent. In the post-war years partly because of rapid growth, more because of inflation, the ratio again fell steadily. In the face of such variety, fixed rules about the permissible level of government debt can have little absolute validity.[8]

The Government has made a serious mistake in seeking to circumscribe the flexibility of fiscal policy in a period of global upheaval by postulating rigid arithmetic rules of this kind.

Supply side measures

In political debate about tackling unemployment, New Labour is liable to give out confusing messages about the role of demand management on the one hand and so-called 'supply-side' measures like training and education on the other. Ministers nearly always speak as if the problem of unemployment is solely a supply-side one and must be tackled by improving work capabilities and skills etc. and by making people on benefit more likely to take up jobs by imposing tougher benefit conditions. The popular presentation of the Government's 'Welfare to Work' measures (to use the American phrase), such as the New Deal and Working Families' Tax Credit, implies that there are plenty of jobs available, and the problem is to make people willing or able to take them. This is clearly at odds with the facts and particularly offensive to those desperate for work in regions where there is a chronic shortage of jobs. What is more it leads to the suggestion (common before the war) that there would be no unemployment problem if only people would stop slacking and go to work.

The more sophisticated reasoning behind this approach (apparent in the small print of Treasury reports) is not that such measures will in themselves create jobs, but that by increasing competition for jobs, pay increases can be held in check with a lower level of unemployment. In other words, the object is to preserve the present balance of power between employers and employed, but with less unemployment – and to enable employers to fill their vacancies and the economy to grow without hitting skills shortages or running into inflationary pressures. The same argument could be used to justify deregulation of the labour market (so-called 'flexibility') and legislation to curb the effective power of the unions. The objection to this approach is that while measures help people into jobs are desirable in themselves, the reliance on keeping the balance of power tipped against employees as a recipe for controlling inflation perpetuates the gross inequalities in society inherited from the Thatcher era.

The Treasury's own figures suggest, moreover, that such policies will have a minuscule effect in reducing the NAIRU or target rate of unemployment. The November 1999 Pre-Budget Report estimated that the Government's labour market measures will increase the proportion of the population of working age in employment by only 0.1 per cent a year. The fact that inflation has remained low despite falling unemployment is probably due mainly to the fact that low inflation itself reduces the pressure for wage increases – the *momentum effect*.

There is an embarrassing discrepancy between Gordon Brown's statements about achieving 'full employment' and the continued suggestions in successive Treasury reports that output and employment were already above the level compatible with the inflation target. Although by post-war standards unemployment was still well above the full employment level, the March 2001 Budget Report suggested that the economy was 'currently operating just above potential', i.e. that unemployment needed to rise, rather than fall any further, to avoid any acceleration in the rate of inflation.[9]

Redefining full employment

How then can we reconcile the fact that the Chancellor and the Prime Minister should be talking about moving towards 'full employment' when there is still such a long way to go, but the Treasury is already worried that unemployment is getting too low for comfort? Is the real answer that Gordon Brown is seeking to redefine 'full employment' to mean something more like the labour market conditions we already have today? He speaks of 'the modern definition of unemployment' as 'employment opportunity for all', and makes great play with the fact that there are now one million unfilled vacancies. There will, of course, always be a pool of unfilled jobs as employers' labour requirements vary and people change jobs or retire. One is bound to treat Gordon Brown's new definition with its emphasis on opportunity with considerable reservations – given his frequent emphasis on *equality of opportunity* rather than *equality of outcome*. After all, the National Lottery is one of the finest examples of equality of opportunity but the odds on winning a prize are pretty slim! There are some fields in which we all need to win. We do not want to see the lottery principle applied to the Health Service or jobs. A job lottery in which we all have equal chances but there are not enough jobs to go round is not the answer. If there are not enough jobs, greater equality of opportunity is not much comfort to those who are unemployed. Nor is it an excuse for blaming them for their plight: someone had to get left out.

The real level of unemployment

Although great play has been made with the fall in the claimant count (those unemployed and claiming benefit) to below one million, we have a long way to go to reach full employment. In February 2001, the Government's own preferred measure, the Labour Force Survey (which includes all those actively seeking work), showed unemployment was still over one and a half million, or 5 per cent of the labour force. But in addition there is considerable hidden unemployment, people who are not officially classified as unemployed but would take up a job if suitable work were available. The Unemployment Unit produces figures for 'broad unemployment' which include people who the Labour Force Survey shows want a job, and are available in two weeks, but are not actively looking for work. In the last quarter of 2000 this stood at 2.2 million.[10]

It is difficult to measure the extent of hidden unemployment. One important group is those on sickness or disability benefit. When unemployment is high, people who are not 100 per cent fit lose their jobs more easily and find it correspondingly difficult to re-enter the labour market. (I remember being taken aback when in the 1980s an employment adviser said, 'Now is the time to raise health standards when you recruit and to weed out staff with poor sickness records.') But when there are plenty of jobs around and labour is scarce, a much higher proportion of those with health problems or disabilities find work. A recent survey showed that half of all male sickness benefit claimants would like a full-time job and over a quarter had looked for work after their last job ended.[11] Such people are not 'fraudsters': they are genuinely suffering from ill-health, and would like to work if suitable jobs were available.

As unemployment increased in the 1980s the number of people on sickness benefits rose sharply; and although it levelled out as unemployment began to fall in the second half of the 1990s, the number on sickness benefits has yet to show any marked reduction. Between 1991 and 1998 the number of benefit claimants of working age incapacitated by long-term sickness or invalidity rose from 0.6 million to 1.9 million, the increase being particularly marked for men. As a result the proportion of the population of working age classified as sick or disabled in 1999 was 7.0 per cent in the UK as against the average of 3.5 per cent for the EU as a whole – despite our lower level of unemployment, 6.2 per cent against an average of 9.5 per cent. If a stronger labour market persists many of these people might be able to get back into work.

Regional unemployment

The weakness of the Government's present approach is particularly apparent in its attitude to regional unemployment. Measures such as the New Deal can be useful in assisting people to get into jobs, provided there are vacancies. Better training may in the longer run encourage firms to expand in areas of chronic unemployment where skilled labour is in short supply. But such 'supply-side' measures are not much use where there are not the jobs to be filled – a situation which still exists in many parts of the country, particularly the older industrial areas in the North. The Government has tried to minimize the regional problem by drawing attention to the fact that there are black spots of heavy localized unemployment all over the country. But although speaking of the regional problem in terms of the 'North-South' divide may be painting the picture with a broad brush, it highlights a fundamental reality. While differences in official unemployment have narrowed in recent years, there are still striking discrepancies between the proportions of people in employment in different regions, particularly among older men. For example, to take the two extremes, in the spring of 2000 70 per cent of men aged from 55 to 64 were in employment in the South East, but only 42 per cent in the North East. There are vast discrepancies in the amount of hidden unemployment between regions. It has been estimated that to bring the proportion of the population of working age employed throughout the UK up to the average of the South would require an additional 1.75 million jobs.[12]

5. RESTORING FULL EMPLOYMENT

Pay and inflation

If we are to restore genuine full employment and not some attenuated new definition of it, fundamental changes in attitude are needed. The economy must no longer be run on the basis that unemployment must be kept above a certain minimum level to limit the bargaining power of labour in under to avoid inflation. The Government should tackle any danger of excessive pay increases in co-operation with the unions and management. It is true that the fragmentation of pay bargaining has made this more difficult than in the past. But the threat of excessive negotiated pay increases rests more with the big battalions than the smaller groups who tend to follow their lead. In talking about 'full employment' again whilst keeping the unions at arms length, the Government has failed to face up to the fact that in the end the fundamental choice is between keeping the wage/price spiral in check by agreement or by the *force majeure* of deliberately maintaining a pool of unemployment. Fighting inflation by agreement was messy but effective until the 1970s, and even in that decade it was more successful than current mythology insists.

The threat of excessive wage increases has not been an issue in New Labour's first term, mainly because they had the good fortune to inherit a low rate of inflation to start with. The strengthening of the pound (and hence falling import prices) also helped – at a heavy cost in terms of damage to manufacturing industry. But any 'shock' from outside, such as another boom in oil prices at a time when sterling was falling, could set off inflationary pressures again. The choice would then be either to resort to deflation and higher unemployment, as in the 1970s, or get agreement with unions and employees to limit wage and price increases. The Government is throwing away a golden opportunity to safeguard against such a danger by getting consultation on such issues in train now, when it would be relatively easy to get agreement.

Throughout the 1980s and 1990s I argued the case for pay policies rather than mass unemployment as the means for avoiding a wage/price spiral.[13] The fact that this approach broke down under the severe strains put on it during the 1970s was no reason to abandon it for all time. The alternative was much worse, if not for the politicians, certainly for those who lost their jobs and industry as a whole. Vast swathes of industrial capacity were wiped out during the 1980s. Today, when inflation no longer seems a serious problem and recession is becoming a greater threat, there may seem little point in returning to the pay policy question. But, on the contrary, taking a long-sighted view, this could be a good moment to put in place arrangements which have every chance of success and would be well established and working smoothly when the next inflationary shock (however it may come) hits us. More fundamentally, entering a new era of 'social partnership' would pave the way for a more egalitarian social atmosphere and restoration of a more acceptable social balance.

Any discussions on pay would need to be set in the context of more general discussions between the Government, unions and employers on economic developments and policy as a whole. A major feature on the agenda should be the future of the manufacturing industry. It is curious that such discussions, which would seem a fairly normal part of a co-operative democratic society, are currently stigmatized by New Labour leaders as 'corporatism' and something to be avoided. There seem to be two (unstated) reasons for this. The first is that bringing the trade unions into such meetings would increase their power and influence. The second is that the less the Government is seen to be in contact with industry, the less likely it is to be involved, or get the blame when things

20

go wrong – although that does not stop it talking to employers. This reading of the political impact of the industrial disputes of the 1970s is not, however, borne out by recent events, such as the crisis on the railways and petrol disputes in the winter of 2000. As with so much of the Government's so-called 'modernization', their reluctance to adopt any form of partnership with the trade unions and employers is actually a regression to pre-war attitudes. The fact that earlier post-war governments of both parties set up arrangements for tripartite consultation, like the National Economic Development Council, does not mean that it is in any sense more advanced or more modern not to do so.

Macro-economic policy

Macro-economic policy should be based on the recognition that both fiscal and monetary policy have a part to play in managing demand. This is particularly important where there is a need to stimulate demand to reduce unemployment. If the UK is threatened with recession, it will be essential for the Chancellor to scrap his 'golden rule' and adopt expansionary Budget measures. He cannot leave it all to the Bank of England. Moreover, if we are to achieve any sort of exchange rate stability, interest rates in the UK cannot differ greatly from those in EMU and elsewhere. Reliance on fiscal rather than monetary policy in the EU will be essential to cope with differences in the macro-economic position in different countries (e.g. faster inflation or higher unemployment). In the extreme case of our joining EMU and sharing a common monetary policy, an active fiscal policy would become the only instrument under national control.

For some time, inflation has no longer been the prime danger facing the world economy, and the deflationary bias inherent in current policies is becoming increasingly inappropriate. If the Bank of England is to retain its independence in setting interest rates, its remit should be widened to include the objectives of achieving a high level of output and employment and a stable and competitive exchange rate, as well as an inflation target. In practice, if it has its feet on the ground, the Monetary Policy Committee must take these factors into account. But this should be formalized to give them more weight.

The so-called 'symmetric' inflation target of 2.5 per cent a year means that the Bank of England must aim not only to prevent the rate of inflation exceeding 2.5 per cent, but also to prevent inflation falling below it. But when inflation is below the target rate, it is nonsensical to pretend that interest rates are really being cut in order to achieve higher inflation. Nobody wants a higher rate of inflation for its own sake. The real reason for reducing interest rates is to avoid a recession and the threat of rising unemployment. (It is particularly inappropriate that those who assert that there is 'no trade-off between inflation and unemployment' should support the concept of a symmetric inflation target – why worry about inflation being below the target rate unless it involves higher unemployment?)

Regional policy

As unemployment has declined, and the scope for further reductions in the more prosperous parts of the country has become limited, the relatively high level of unemployment in other regions has become one of the main obstacles to achieving something approaching full employment. It must be recognized that the continued existence of relatively heavy unemployment in certain parts of the country is due to a shortage of jobs, rather than the inability or unwillingness of people to take them. A key element in any policy to achieve full employment must be to increase the demand for labour in the relatively depressed areas. One essential need is to ensure that the pound is kept at a competitive level. The devastating effects of the overvalued pound on industries like motors and steel is only too evident. A competitive pound is essential for manufacturing industry in all parts of the country. But in the longer term, given the need to avoid over-heating the South, strengthening the demand for labour in the North depends on the use of measures which are essentially discriminatory – in particular strengthening the incentives for industry to expand in these areas. The problem will not be solved, as the Government often seems to suggest, simply by encouraging the Regional Development Agencies to develop their own regions. While this is desirable in itself, it will not necessarily remove the differences between the prosperous and hard-hit areas. It may in fact widen them.

Greater emphasis needs to be placed on attracting industries to the affected areas by improving the incentives for industry to invest there. Although government policy on regional incentives for industrial development is heavily circumscribed by EU rules, there is considerable scope for strengthening the present discretionary incentives. Our report on *Tackling the Regional Jobs Gap* proposed that all new manufacturing investment should receive an automatic grant of, say, 25 per cent of the cost in the worst affected (so-called 'Tier 1') areas and 15 per cent in other ('Tier 2') areas of heavy unemployment, with discretionary top-up grants in special cases.[14] In addition, greater use should be made of the present system of discretionary grants to encourage new investment in business services and high technology firms in these areas.

The wider context

The UK economy cannot, however, be considered in isolation. It is highly dependent on the state of demand in the rest of the EU and other major trading partners. We are also increasingly vulnerable to developments in global financial markets. The need to get away from the present neo-liberal consensus and devise new and more effective policies for achieving growth and prosperity in the European Union and the world economy as a whole is discussed in chapters 4 and 5.

Notes

1. Reproduced in *Unemployment: A Labour Policy* (Labour Party, 1921).
2. Stewart, M., *The Jekyll and Hyde Years: Politics and Economic Policy since 1964* (Dent, 1987).
3. Skidelsky, R., *Thatcherism* (Chatto and Windus, 1988), and Jenkins, P., *Mrs Thatcher's Revolution* (Cape, 1987).
4. Thatcher, M., *The Downing Street Years* (Harper Collins, 1993).
5. Friedman, M., *The Role of Monetary Policy*, American Economic Review no. 58 (1968).
6. *Report on Economic and Monetary Union in the Economic Community* (European Community, 1989).
7. *Pre-Budget Report* (November 1997).
8. Dow, J.C.R., *Major Recessions* (Oxford University Press, 1998).
9. *Budget 2001* (March 2001).
10. *Working brief*, Unemployment Unit, March 2001.

11. Beatty, C. and Fothergill, S., *Incapacity Benefit and Unemployment* (Centre for Regional Economic and Social Research, Sheffield Hallam University, 1999).
12. *Tackling the Regional Jobs Gap*, Report of a Working Party on Regional Economic Policy (Employment Policy Institute and Alliance for Regional Aid, 2000).
13. For example, *Pay Strategy for the 1990s* (IPPR 1990).
14. *Tackling the Regional Jobs Gap*.

Chapter 2

A FAIRER SOCIETY

All inequality that has no special utility to justify it is injustice.

Jeremy Bentham

1. SOCIAL JUSTICE

The rise in unemployment in the 1980s and the ascendancy of the Thatcherite ethos led to a dramatic increase in inequality. Between 1981–3 and 1991–3 the share of total incomes going to the most well-off tenth of the population rose by nearly one-quarter – from 21 per cent to 26 per cent – whereas the share of the poorest tenth went down by nearly one-third from 4 per cent to just under 3 per cent.[1] During the first half of the 1990s the distribution of income remained relatively stable, but there appears to have been a further smaller increase in inequality towards the end of the decade. With the exception of Portugal and Greece, by the mid-1990s the UK had the most unequal income distribution in the EU.[2] There was a similar increase in the inequality of distribution of capital. Whereas in 1981 the wealthiest 10 per cent of the population owned 56 per cent of marketable wealth (excluding housing), by 1991 they owned 64 per cent.[3]

Reducing these vast inequalities in income and wealth should be a major objective of any civilized government. But New Labour has been strangely reluctant to acknowledge the reduction of these inequalities as an explicit objective. Despite some 'stealthy' redistribution in his Budgets, Gordon Brown, for example, makes great play with the suggestion that New Labour have replaced Old Labour's touchstone of 'equality' with their new concept of 'equality of opportunity' – a phrase Margaret Thatcher was very fond of. But equality of opportunity is only part of the answer. The distribution of rewards must be fair, as well as the chance to earn them. Greater equality of opportunity will not in itself necessarily lead to any greater equality of income. Indeed, a 'meritocratic' society may be one in which greater inequality is regarded as justified. As Michael Young wrote in his satirical sketch of British society in 2033, *The Rise of the Meritocracy*:

> Now that people are classified by ability, the gap between the classes has inevitably become wider... Today, the elite know that, except for a grave error in administration, which should at once be corrected if brought to light, their social inferiors are inferiors in other ways as well – that is in the two vital qualities of intelligence and education...[4]

The causation is the other way round: a more egalitarian and classless society is an essential condition for anything like equality of opportunity to exist. Great disparities in parents' incomes inevitably give some children a much better chance in life than others. Moreover, if people's opportunities in life are to depend less and less on their parents' income and background and more on their own ability, increasing numbers of children from working-class homes will get what are traditionally regarded as middle-class jobs; and conversely more children from middle-class homes will have to be content with working-class jobs. Accountants and lawyers will have to accept it as perfectly normal if they have sons or daughters who become chefs or plumbers, and not feel that their children are failures because they are not following in their parents' footsteps. True equality of opportunity will only be a reality in a relatively classless and egalitarian society.

Equality

Although equality (shades of the French Revolution) has been regarded as a major tenet of Labour and other left-wing parties, this has always been an over-simplification in the economic field. When it comes to the distribution of income, the objective has been to remove the injustice of excessive inequality, rather than to achieve absolute equality. So far as Labour's supporters are concerned, for most people the objection to the present distribution of income and wealth is that it is not 'fair', rather than that it is not 'equal'. The emphasis on equality was, however, a long-standing feature of Fabian socialism and rested heavily on R.H. Tawney's *Equality*, first published in 1931.[5] Tawney's vigorous attack on social injustice in all its forms was coupled with a powerful case for redistributive taxation to finance a major extension in social services and public ownership to control the inevitable concentration of economic power. With Harold Laski and Douglas Jay, Tawney provided the basic arguments for much of the programme of the 1945 Labour government.

Tawney was, however, much more careful than some of his latter-day apostles in clarifying the practical application of equality, as indeed was Tony Crosland. Tawney wrote:

> While diversities of income, corresponding to varieties of function and capacity, would survive, they would neither be heightened by capricious inequalities of circumstance and opportunity, nor perpetuated from generation to generation by the institution of inheritance. Differences of remuneration between different individuals might remain; contrasts between the civilization of different classes would vanish.

Income and work

One fascinating reason why Fabian authors like Bernard Crick and Raymond Plant placed such total reliance on the simple concept of equality, rather than the more complex one of fairness, is that they tended to ignore the relation between income and work. For example, when the Fabian Society celebrated its centenary in 1984 with a volume of *Fabian Essays in Socialist Thought*[6] it was remarkable that throughout the discussion of equality in these essays there was no mention of income as a reward for work. Indeed the word 'work' was conspicuous by its absence. In this the authors follow a similar omission in Rawls' *A Theory of Justice*,[7] whose influence they acknowledge. (I suspect that this may be because academics see no hard and fast line between work and leisure or any direct relation between their work and their pay!) Their approach seems to be that there is a pool of output or income to be distributed; it should be distributed as equally as possible; but some residual inequality may be required to provide the incentives needed to keep the economic system going.

A more generally acceptable idea is that those who work make an identifiable contribution to the pool of goods and services available for distribution, and their income should be based on this contribution. In other words the starting point is that people should get a fair return for their work. Most people who work believe that they should get paid more for harder work and also for 'better' work, although what constitutes 'better' work is always debatable. The idea that people in charge should get more than those under them also runs very deep. These common-sense and universally held propositions form part of a deep-felt desire for a just pattern of rewards, held not least in the trade union movement. The old Clause IV of the Labour Party's Constitution, despite its Marxist resonances, took a more realistic view, stating the aim as being 'To secure for workers by hand or by brain the full fruits of their industry and the most equitable distribution thereof that may be possible...': note 'equitable', not 'equal'.

The trade unions are very concerned about fairness and relativities in pay, but by no stretch of the imagination do they, or did they, accept simple equality (as opposed to less inequality) as the guiding concept. It was thus paradoxical that those who sought to articulate a political philosophy for a party originally based on the trade union movement should have taken the concept of equality as the key to that philosophy, rather than the more complex one of fairness or social justice – or, as the 1945 Labour manifesto put it, *Fair Shares For All*. The appeal of greater social justice is a strong one. The desire for fair play lies deep in us all, and unfairness or injustice generate strong emotional objections whether it be within the home, at work or in society at large.

The danger of taking equality as the key criterion was that those who did so tended to be equally unsympathetic to differences in income that were economically or socially justified as to those that were not. Anything that reduced income differentials was reckoned desirable. Tax policy and differences in pay were sometimes judged solely on this basis. But building workers on overtime or people who have spent their evenings getting further qualifications do not see it this way. Such an approach left no place for the concept of well-earned rewards and implicitly supported the view that the steeper the burden of income tax the better. In the end what was regarded as Labour's failure to regard any sizeable income as 'legitimate', whatever the economic contribution on which it was based, provoked the Thatcherite response, which was to regard *any* level of income or wealth as self-justifying. The real question should be: have they earned it?

I believe that the essential objective that the left has always been trying to articulate is that of a 'fairer' society, in particular, the pursuit of economic and social justice. This would, of course, involve a marked reduction in the present degree of inequality in all its aspects. Such an approach would clearly put at the top of the political agenda the greatest unfairness of all – the lack of jobs for all those who want to work. It would also encompass all those issues of social injustice in terms of access to education and health that have always been key issues on Labour's political agenda.

Income distribution

The pursuit of a fairer society goes beyond questions of redistribution through taxation or social security benefits. It raises more fundamental issues of the distribution of income and wealth *before* tax. The left has not yet started to get to grips with the longer-term issues of distribution of income and wealth now that large-scale public ownership is no longer on the agenda. The traditional socialist belief in public ownership had two strands. One was that state ownership would be both more socially responsible and more efficient – for example, in providing an efficient rail system or rationalizing the steel industry. The second strand was the idea that a socialist society would do away with vast holdings of private wealth and disparities in income. The larger the public sector, the greater would be the scope for lessening inequalities of income and wealth.

In the event, however, the gradualist path of piecemeal nationalization with fair compensation was concerned almost entirely with social responsibility and efficiency, rather than greater equality as such. But even if public ownership did not immediately bring greater equality, it was a prerequisite for it. The pattern of incomes in the public sector was less unequal. Nationalized industry chairmen got paid a lot less than their private sector counterparts – as we saw in reverse with privatization. In the first three years after privatization, directors' salaries in British Aerospace, British Telecom, Cable and Wireless, Enterprise Oil and British Airways doubled or trebled.[8]

The abandonment of public ownership as part of Labour Party policy raises the need to consider critically the distribution of income and wealth in a largely privately owned economy. The market does not necessarily lead to either a fair or an efficient pattern of rewards. The level of bonuses for company directors and the City elite is widely regarded as greedy and offensive. Is it really good for the British economy that a young banker should be paid so much more than a fully qualified engineer? Embracing the market for goods is one thing; embracing the market for labour is another. We need to re-examine the social institutions and arrangements which determine what people earn, accumulate or inherit. This involves a very wide range of issues, such as equal pay and opportunities, the minimum wage, Pay Review Boards, the determination of top managers' salaries, the status of employees in company law, occupational pension schemes and much else besides. Reconsidering such issues in the context of establishing a fairer society is an essential step in reformulating the left's political philosophy and agenda.

2. THE BALANCE OF POWER

A key factor in determining the distribution of incomes is the balance of power in the economy. The essence of the current approach to economic policy is to maintain something like the existing balance of power between employers and unions in order to avoid inflationary pay settlements. This in itself may seem reasonable enough, but the wider implications are less acceptable. The strength of the demand for labour not only affects pay negotiations but also, equally important, it affects the way people are treated. For example, when labour became plentiful, so-called labour 'flexibility' meant that people were compelled to work longer hours or extra shifts at their employers' discretion. The scandalous 'zero hours contract' was introduced under which people had to be on standby all the week but might end up with no paid work. On the other hand, when labour is scarce and difficult to recruit, employers have to take more heed of their staff and make more effort to allow their employees to work flexible hours to help them meet the needs of their families – for example, to take time off when children are ill. Mrs Thatcher wanted to restore the 'right to manage' – but, as Beveridge said 50 years ago:

> The challenge to management that will be presented by full employment is a challenge that enlightened employers will welcome. The essence of civilization is that men should come to be led more by hope and ambition and less by fear.[9]

As well as affecting the balance of power between employers and employed, full employment had wider consequences for the general balance and nature of society. The virtual abolition of domestic service during and after the war was a case in point. It was just one symptom of a more egalitarian society. For only when there are considerable differences in incomes can people in one section of the community afford to employ others in this way on a one-to-one basis. Less directly, the greater equality of rewards in the post-war years reflected a more egalitarian climate of opinion in which the award of astronomical bonuses to top executives was virtually out of the question.

The abandonment of full employment in the 1980s had disproportionate effects on those with the fewest skills or educational qualifications, or with poor health or disabilities. Employers in any walk of life recruit the best people they can get. When labour is plentiful, they set their sights higher, irrespective of the precise requirements of the jobs. The consequence is that not only does unemployment fall most heavily on those at the bottom of the employment ladder, but wages and conditions at the bottom deteriorate. It is not that there is a 'shortage of unskilled jobs', as is often suggested, but that the unskilled lose out in the fight for the available jobs. As a result the pay of those at the bottom of the pile is depressed by the competition for jobs and inequalities are wider. The growing disparity of pay in different occupations is illustrated by the fact that over the last 20 years men's pay in the highest paid categories has risen nearly one-third faster than that of those in the lowest paid categories. There was a similar pattern for women, with the disparity rather less than that for men in the 1980s but the same in the 1990s.[10]

3. INDUSTRY AND SOCIAL PARTNERSHIP

The retreat from full employment in the 1980s, and the shift in power from workers to employers as labour became easier to recruit, not only led to greater inequality of incomes but had a profound effect throughout industry. It has encouraged a more autocratic and less consensual approach to management. Working conditions have in many cases deteriorated. New forms of casual employment have thrived. Under the Thatcher government this process was reinforced by measures to reduce worker protection.

Employers' attitudes to consultation with their workforce are very sensitive to the state of the labour market. It is no coincidence that the abandonment of full employment coincided with a general retreat from joint consultation and all forms of worker participation. When labour was scarce and the unions stronger, there was a greater incentive for employers to consult and cooperate with employees. After a brief flirtation with 'social partnership', New Labour has shown no interest in encouraging such consultation. Indeed it has resisted EU moves that would entitle employees to be consulted in advance about closures and redundancies.

The ascendancy of the financial ethos

In recent years the growing power of financial markets has led to a marked change in the environment in which industrial managers have to operate. Industry has always had to pay heed to its financial backers, particularly when it needs additional finance. In the past, however, shareholders could in many respects be treated as a necessary evil, to be handled tactfully at annual meetings. Today, not merely the shareholders as such but also those who trade in shares are regarded as the all-powerful authority to be placated. The consequence has been the spread of the now familiar disease of 'short-termism' with seriously adverse effects on the health of industry. While similar trends have been operating world-wide, particularly in the US, not all countries have been affected to the same extent. Japan and Germany, in particular, have preserved much of their former industrial culture; and continental Europe has for the most part preserved its commitment to social partnership. New

Labour at one point seemed about to make social partnership a key part of its appeal under the flag of 'stakeholding', but it is now vigorously criticizing its EU partners' adherence to social partnership and trying to force the so-called Anglo-Saxon model down their throats.

The danger today is that the financial ethos is gaining universal ascendancy to the detriment of successful industrial management. Press comment is dominated by the views of financial markets. Day-to-day movements in share prices can even lead to decisions to close plants and fire workers, which should rest on much longer-term considerations. Before we can even consider the possibility of wider goals for companies, we need to liberate industry from the domination of financial markets and the shallow short-termism that goes with it.

Industry is being made increasingly unstable by the growth of takeovers. The financial markets have a vested interest in promoting such activities, whether or not there is any strategic justification for them, because of the vast fees to be earned and the changes in share prices involved. In so far as there is any substance in the idea that the threat of a takeover keeps management on its toes, it puts further emphasis on maintaining share prices in the short term, rather than concentrating on long-run industrial success.

Similar considerations apply to the spread of share option schemes for top management. Management incentive schemes should be linked to long-term profitability rather than share prices – particularly as the movement in share prices in most companies is more sensitive to the short-term behaviour of the stock market than the performance of that particular company.

The insidious invasion of the short-term financial culture has had a greater effect on the prevailing ethos in industry than privatization. To take the steel industry again as an example: before, during and after nationalization, there was a deep commitment to the industry reinforced by the fact that many people spent the whole of their working lives in it. Management thought of itself as the custodian of a well-defined industry with its people, its technology and plant. Their job was to make the most of these assets and establish a flourishing iron and steel industry.

The closures by Corus, the Anglo-Dutch steel company, announced in February 2001, illustrated vividly the victory of financial over industrial thinking. The British steel industry had been having a hard time because the over-valuation of the pound was both hitting its customers in engineering and car production and making British steel less competitive in Europe. But the capacity and skills involved had been built up over many years, and once closed, the plants involved are unlikely ever to be reopened or replaced. Decisions as to their future should have reflected a long-term strategy for the company, not a temporary blip in the level of sterling. Apart from stemming current losses, the decision seems to have been precipitated by a desire to drive up the share price. The financial community duly applauded the cutbacks, whilst ministers stood on the sidelines helplessly, and those who worked in the industry and the communities they lived in were devastated. But the attitude of the Corus management now is: 'We are here to make money, not steel.'

Stakeholding

In distinction to the prevailing short-term financial ethos, the essence of the stakeholder approach is that in formulating company policy, management must take into account not only the interests of shareholders, but also those of its employees, customers, suppliers and the communities in which it operates. This has been a long-standing concept in business strategy, arousing strong controversy between those who believe that businesses should concentrate solely on their legal obligation to maximize returns to their shareholders, and those who believe that wider interests must be taken into account.[11] Those in the latter group range from the realists, who say that in practice every firm has to take some account of other interests of this kind, to the reformers, such as David Marquand and Will Hutton,[12] who see the stakeholding concept as a platform for a new role for the company in the community – with company law adjusted to take this into account.

The hard-nosed purists argue that only profit is objectively measurable and to bring in other objectives means ending up in a quagmire of conflicting values. On the other hand, most industrial managers – as opposed to business school writers – know that in real life they have to take a variety of non-quantifiable factors and competing objectives into account in taking decisions. The real issue is the *relative weight* to be attached to the respective objectives and values of the various stakeholders. For example, whereas for many years the question of pollution has had to be taken into account (if only to satisfy legal requirements), more recently pressure from the environmental lobbies has ensured that environmental considerations have to be given much greater weight – if only for PR reasons. On a different plane, British firms have generally fought shy of accepting overt responsibility for such things as city centre development, housing and schools, as some large American corporations have done. On this side of the Atlantic such schemes seem reminiscent of the company town, and for a long time such social activities have been regarded as the province of democratically elected local (or national) government.

There are two different areas of debate about the extent to which the drive for profit should be mitigated by consideration for the interests of the workers in the company and those outside with whom it deals. One is how far taking into account these interests will in the long run benefit the firm and ensure its survival, to the eventual benefit of the shareholders. The other issue is whether, or to what extent, these interests should receive such benefit even at the expense of the shareholders. Taking into account stakeholders' interests generally means taking a longer-term view than short-term profit maximization would dictate. The need to establish good long-term relations with the company's customers and suppliers is virtually axiomatic. The company must also take a long-term view of its workforce if it is to develop their skills and loyalty – though unfortunately there are many firms who do not think in these terms. Again the investment decisions that companies have to make are inevitably long term – as is expenditure on research and development. In capital intensive industries, like chemicals, it takes a period of years to design, build and commission new plant, which then needs, say, 20 years of working life if it is to be economic. The need to take a long-term view is an essential feature of a successful industrial culture, as opposed to the short-term horizons of most financial activity. There is a deep divide between the day-to-day, or hour-to-hour, profit-making ethos of the financial dealer and the longer-term horizon characteristic of effective industrial management.

The long-term industrial approach underlies prevailing attitudes in two of the most successful industrial countries in the post-war era: Germany and Japan. (The fact that Japan is suffering a macro-economic crisis of inadequate demand, and its financial sector is in a mess, does not detract from the fact that in industrial terms Japanese firms are in the top league.) Ronald Gore has referred to the Anglo-Saxon (predominately US and UK) model and the German-Japanese model as *Stock Market Capitalism* and *Welfare Capitalism* respectively.[13] Despite pressure to conform with the American model, there are still very substantial differences between the two.

Dore describes the difference between the culture of the Japanese and British firm as that between the 'stakeholder' and 'shareholder' firm or the employee-favouring firm versus the shareholder-favouring firm. Japanese firms 'are not seen as anybody's property. They are more like communities... Their primary concern is the reputation of the community and the welfare of its members.' The emphasis is on shared membership of the community rather than an implicitly adversarial contrast between managers and workers, and the unions that represent them. Managers' main objective is the long-term prosperity of the firm rather than short-term profitability or share prices. When they are faced with the problems of a declining industry, Japanese managers seek to transfer the maximum possible number of employees to new activities rather than to liquidate loss-making decisions as soon as possible, thereby making employees redundant. The Japanese have a smaller dispersion of rewards and no distinction between wage and salary earners, with less emphasis on cash rewards for success.

In Germany, the keynote is 'co-determination', with a legal framework governing the relations between shareholders, managers and workers. German firms have both a supervisory board and a management board. In the coal and steel industries (which were the first to be regulated) employee representatives have half the seats on the supervisory board, with a chairman elected by board members. In other large firms (with over 2,000 employees) shareholders have the same number of delegates as employees but elect the chairman. In firms with between 500 and 2,000 employees, employee representatives are entitled to one-third of the seats on the board. All firms with more than 500 employees must have works councils – one in each establishment and a central council for the firm. For smaller firms these are not legal requirements, but many of them also have works councils.

The more cohesive industrial systems in Japan and Germany have come under pressure for change in recent years with the growing ascendancy of the financial ethos in the Anglo-Saxon world. Given that the future of industry in Europe and North America will depend to an important extent on the successful development of high technology, the need is to maintain or establish an environment in which firms can take the longer-term view needed for such developments. This is something financial markets are quite incapable of doing, as the recent boom and bust in so-called 'dotcom' shares made plain.

Company law reform

How can we end the growing domination of British industry by finance and ensure that companies take into account wider considerations than the short-term interests of the shareholders? The key to the problem is the need for a fundamental change in social and political attitudes. Firms are necessarily sensitive abut their public reputations, and in so far as the climate of public opinion makes it important for them to pay more heed to, say, environmental considerations, they will start to do so. But as the environmental case makes clear, public opinion needs to be backed up where possible by appropriate legislation – or monitoring by unofficial or official bodies. The reform of company law is overdue. Although the basis of traditional company law is conceptually out of date, it has survived so long mainly because the provisions have been loose and flexible enough to provide a formal structure for companies which may in effect be run in such a way as to reflect a recognition of wider interests. But the time has now come to spell out formally the duty of companies to take into account the interests of their employees, customers, suppliers and the community as well as their shareholders.

A key point in any new company legislation is the structure and composition of the board. The most specific issue is employee representation at board level. The post-war movement for greater employee participation peaked with the appointment of the Commission on Industrial Democracy, chaired by Lord Bullock, which reported in 1977. The majority report (not signed by the employer members) made proposals for trade union directors to sit on the boards of companies employing

37

2,000 or more people.[14] Even the minority report (put forward by the business members) advocated supervisory boards made up of equal numbers of workers, shareholders and independent representatives. The Report, however, evoked strong opposition from employers, and the whole subject was quickly buried when Mrs Thatcher came to power in 1979. Since then it has not been effectively reopened – or only in passing when the idea of stakeholding briefly held sway.

Making employee participation at board level mandatory for all large companies would be the most effective way of ensuring that management worked in co-operation with their staff and not in any arbitrary or dictatorial fashion. It would also create an atmosphere in which employees would see that their views on the operation of the company and its future were being heard. When employee representation was last on the public agenda in the 1970s, the trade unions took a strong line that the number of worker and management directors should be equal with some additional outside directors, who would have in effect a casting vote. This was accepted by the Bullock Committee. But boards do not work by voting, rather by seeking the nearest they can get to consensus. It is the calibre of the employee directors on a board, not the number, that is important.

An alternative approach would be to adopt the German system involving a two-tier structure of managing and supervisory boards with trade unions and community representatives on the supervisory board. This is part of a generally more consultative approach for large companies in the EU. Whilst such a two-tier structure is generally regarded as foreign to British company law, it is not very far from the *de facto* position in some large companies, which have an executive board or committee comprising the full-time managing directors as well as the company board with outside members. The difference lies in the fact that the executive committee has no statutory position or responsibilities.

It is time to reopen the debate on the future of the company. In doing so we should welcome, rather than reject, the concept of social partnership still flourishing in the EU. There is nothing outrageously radical in recognizing the right of all those who work in a firm to have an influence on policy and have their interests treated with respect. It is symptomatic of the ascendancy of the Thatcherite consensus over the embryonic Third Way that these various ideas fundamental to the concept of stakeholding should have virtually disappeared from public debate.

4. THE PUBLIC SECTOR

Public ownership

Until the 1980s, discussion about the structure of industry concentrated on the debate between public and private ownership. This was the most obvious area to which the post-war political consensus did not extend. To Labour the case for nationalization was partly a matter of socialist principle and partly empirical. At the end of the war the case for amalgamating the four railway companies and running them as one public system was widely accepted. So too was the case for running electricity generation as an integrated national system. The wheel may now have turned full circle. The chaos in the railways in the winter of 2000–1 has seriously damaged public confidence in the arguments for breaking up the system into a variety of companies. If the electricity generating system finds itself unable to cope with peak demands in a severe winter, as has happened in Auckland and California, then electricity privatization will also come under fire. Again in the case of the London Underground, any residual support for the proposed fragmentation of the Tube under PPP is rapidly evaporating.

The most controversial nationalization was that of steel – the only industry to be denationalized and then renationalized. A major part of the case for steel nationalization was the generally recognized need to rationalize the industry – something industry leaders in the British Iron and Steel Federation had been trying to do since before the war. It was only in the 1970s when the 14 major steel companies were merged into the publicly-owned British Steel Corporation, that the overdue modernization of the industry could take place. Over 30 outdated Open Hearth steel-making plants were closed down and replaced by five large oxygen steel-making plants.

The nationalized industries also tended to adopt a more inclusive style of management than their private sector counterparts. This was particularly marked in the case of the British Steel Corporation which from the start had employee directors on its divisional boards and for a crucial time also on its main board. My own experience of this experiment as a senior manager in the Corporation was extremely positive. The worker directors had a difficult task, combining a shop floor job and managerial meetings, but as experienced lay officials in their unions, and very often active in local government, they were well fitted to the task. (It was noticeable that at the annual Corporation conferences the worker directors were often more effective in getting their points across than the managers!) It is significant that this massive restructuring of the industry was achieved with the eventual agreement and co-operation of the unions, thanks partly to the enabling role of the worker directors. Admittedly the steel industry was fertile ground for such an experiment in that it had a long history of good industrial relations, but it is tragic that this was brought to an end with privatization and (with the exception of a brief trial in the Post Office) has not been repeated elsewhere. In the words of the worker directors' own summing up of their experience at the time:

> Ultimately the worker director debate is a question of power-sharing. Are shareholders and managers willing to devolve power to their employees? Are workers ready to receive power? The first question now hangs in the balance. The answer to the second by the British Steel Corporation employee directors is an unshakeable 'Yes.'[15]

New public enterprise

In considering the objectives of industrial enterprises, there is a spectrum of different types of enterprise ranging from the local restaurant, which everyone is perfectly content to see run on a purely commercial basis, to public utilities like water, electricity and railways, where it is generally agreed the prime objective should be to provide a public service. The former consensus that such utilities should be publicly owned was largely based on the idea that this would ensure that the public interest was put first. The objective of putting public service first was more clear-cut under public ownership, than in the case of private ownership with the pursuit of profit tempered by public regulation. This was particularly important where the utility concerned was effectively a monopoly.

The process of privatization in some cases involved breaking up monopolies to introduce competition (as in the case of telecommunications) or even fragmentation for its own sake, as in the case of the railways and London Underground. But in the case of water, which is a natural monopoly, the undertakings have simply been transferred from the public to the private sector. It is not clear how far the consumers' apparent benefits from price competition in the case of telecoms, electricity and gas represent improved efficiency or merely price cutting, which the regulator could have achieved by tighter regulation. But in the case of the fragmentation of the railways and London Underground, efficiency and the consumer have suffered severely. Regulation, rather than unified management, is not an effective way of dealing with private industrial organizations which need to work more closely together. This has brought the question of public ownership back into public discussion.

The wave of privatization by the Conservative government in the 1980s ruled out of court any reconsideration of the structure of the existing nationalized industries. There was a case for giving them more room to manoeuvre, and greater freedom to raise capital, without wholesale transfer to the private sector. This applied particularly to an industry like steel, where freedom to move into forward integration into processing industries and distribution (like most competing companies) would have been valuable. But even in the case of public utilities like gas or telecoms similar arguments applied. In the latter case, the basic problem (which was never properly addressed) was how to ensure that such organizations put the public interest first without excessive and stultifying departmental control. This would have required major changes in the statutes under which they operated. Giving them freedom to issue bonds and raise their own capital would have been a major step in this direction. Study is needed of alternative, more appropriate, forms of organization for the public utilities and transport industries than the ordinary public company supervised by the regulator, but with greater flexibility than the former nationalized industries. This is most urgent in the transport field.

PFI/PPP

The Tory government's measures to privatize and introduce private capital into the provision of public services – the Public Finance Initiative (PFI) – were originally based on the idea that private sector management was inherently more efficient than that in the public sector; so that even though the cost of capital to private firms was bound to be higher than the cost of government borrowing, the net effect would be a reduction in costs. An additional advantage was that this would reduce the PSBR and the volume of public debt – even though, of course, the volume of public sector assets would be correspondingly reduced. Despite its criticisms when in opposition, the New Labour government continued and enhanced the PFI, rechristening it PPP, Public-Private Partnerships. PPP is now in danger of putting public investment in double jeopardy by resorting to private financing of public services in cases where the cost of capital will not only be higher, but the management of the service provided will also be clearly less efficient, as the disastrous chaos on the railways in the winter of 2000 has illustrated. The future of the London Underground service is a further worrying example. Even the *Financial Times* urged the Government to 'drop this ill-conceived project'.[16]

It is time for a fundamental reconsideration of the case for injecting private sector finance into public sector investment projects, e.g. in building hospitals or schools. In doing so, it is essential to distinguish at least three different issues. The first is the argument that relying on private finance to fund such projects reduces government borrowing and makes it possible to carry out schemes 'for which the money would not otherwise be available'. Whilst widely used, not least in government circles, it is clear on closer examination that there is no justification for this assertion. The essential reason for keeping down public borrowing is to avoid having to raise taxes in order to pay the interest on it. But if such projects are financed by private borrowing, although public debt is nominally lower, the Treasury still has to find the money to pay whoever undertook the project enough to cover their interest charges – charges incurred at a higher rate of interest than the government itself would have borne. In the end the Government is liable to pay more in service charges than it would have paid out in interest if it had financed the scheme itself. In such cases, the supposed advantage is purely presentational: public sector borrowing requirements and public debt are lower, but the future burden on the taxpayer will be higher. There is no advantage to the public purse in using private finance for public investment projects unless this results in savings in construction costs which would more than cover the higher interest rate costs. The pressure to keep down public debt, irrespective of the consequences, has, however, become an article of faith in the New Orthodoxy. It is enshrined in the EU Stability and Growth Pact and in Gordon Brown's own budgetary rules.

A similar fallacy dominates the question of allowing public bodies like the London Underground to issue bonds to finance investment. If they are formally guaranteed by the government, they are classified as public debt; if they are not guaranteed, they are not so classified – although in practice the distinction is of little economic significance. The real burden of such investment on the economy is the same, however they are financed.

The second issue is whether private sector management of construction projects is inherently more efficient. If it is, the answer is not necessarily to resort to private finance: the project can be publicly financed but managed by private consultants. There is, however, in fact no reason why public sector managers should not manage construction projects as efficiently as their private counterparts if given the necessary facilities. In fact public sector managers managing, say, hospital projects would be able to gain more specialized expertise than private sector managers covering a much wider field. If there had not been such a bias towards private sector involvement, this would have been the first line of attack.

The third issue concerns private/public projects where the private contractor remains responsible for some aspects of the project after the construction is completed: i.e. the contract is to supply so many hospital beds etc. for 30 years rather than merely construct the hospital. That this is becoming increasingly prevalent is shown by the fact that capital expenditure forms on average little over one-fifth of the total cost of PFI projects.[17] But is it sensible in the longer run for hospital managers, or education authorities, to be tied down by long-term supply contracts of this kind? They may well find that as time goes by they need to alter the arrangements, which they would do in a straightforward way if the management of the building etc. were directly subject to their own control, but which involves the hassle and expense of revising contracts when the facilities are partly managed by a private contractor.

There is little doubt that the Treasury is ideologically wedded to the use of private finance on the grounds that it keeps down public expenditure in the short run; even though the eventual cost to the public purse may be higher. A Government which was genuinely open-minded as to whether to use public or private finance would be much more critical of the assumption that the private sector can manage everything better, and would give more weight to the fact that running public utilities in the public interest is not the natural function of private enterprise – particularly in an age where the shareholders' short-term interests are the dominant factor dictating management decisions.

5. PAYING FOR PUBLIC SERVICES

If there is scope for new combinations of private and public enterprise in fields like transport and power, does the same apply to health and education? Here there are two issues. The first whether these services should be universally available free of cost – even though some people may prefer to pay for private health insurance or education. The second issue is whether the providers of free education and health services should remain public institutions subject to democratic control.

If there is to be any pretext of achieving a fairer society and equality of opportunity, state-financed, free provision of these services at a good standard is absolutely essential. At the moment, at any rate, this is an almost universally held view – save in the case of university education. But when it comes to the actual provision, increasing reliance is being placed on private suppliers, e.g. companies contracting to run schools for local authorities, or NHS links with the private health sector, and Labour's election manifesto suggested that this process would accelerate. The use of profit-making companies to run local authority schools or NHS hospitals should be viewed with considerable suspicion. Education and health have always been fields where public or charitable enterprise has been the driving force, rather than the profit motive, and this should remain the case. There is not inherent reason why, given adequate resources, public sector bodies cannot provide a high standard of service.

Education and health

If, however, state education and the National Health Service are to provide a universal service at a level which is acceptable to us all, we must be prepared to pay the taxes needed to finance them. Both major parties are dodging this issue. The provision of improved education, health and other public services raises long-term tax issues which need better informed public discussion. This is inhibited by the way in which the Treasury currently presents its expenditure forecasts in terms of so-called 'real' increases in expenditure – all part of their addiction to Stonewall Jackson's dictum: 'Mystify, mislead and surprise.' If prices are forecast to rise by 2.5 per cent a year and they are allowing an increase of, say, 4.5 per cent in expenditure on education, they refer to this as an increase of 2 per cent in 'real terms'. This gives the impression that 2 per cent a year more resources are being devoted to education, for example in a 2 per cent increase in the number of teachers. This is not the case. For with the assumption that productivity is increasing by 2 per cent a year in *the economy as a whole*, the Government's 2.5 per cent inflation target is consistent with an average increase in pay of 4.5 per cent – this is the guideline the Bank of England takes in deciding whether the rise in earnings is consistent with achieving the inflation target. But in services like education or health there is (unlike industry) very little room for similar increases in productivity. We look for *fewer* pupils per teacher, or patients per nurse, not *more*. But if teachers and nurses are to get the same sort of annual pay rises as other people (i.e. around 4.5 per cent), an increase in spending of 4.5 per cent will merely cover a constant number of them. In any meaningful sense there has been no increase in the real resources denoted to education and health. Education has merely become more expensive relative to factory-made goods.

The more the public sector is confined to the provision of services of this kind, the more important this becomes. We have to face the fact that merely to provide the same standard of service would mean that public expenditure in these fields must rise in line with national income. But in addition, there is strong pressure not merely to maintain but to improve the standard of services. Indeed public demand for improved health, education and other public services is to be expected as living standards improve. This means that expenditure on them must increase as a proportion of national income. Current discussion of public expenditure plans and the 'growing burden of taxation' completely fail to take this into account. Political debate is couched in terms of which party can keep public expenditure to the lower proportion of national income and hence provide the lowest level of taxation. Only the Liberal Democrats, to their credit, have come out openly in favour of higher taxation and better services.

The Institute of Fiscal Studies have produced the following comparison of changes in public spending under Tony Blair's Government, with those under Margaret Thatcher and John Major:[18]

Average annual increase in 'real expenditure' (actual or planned) per cent

	Thatcher years	Major years	Blair years*
Education	1.2	2.1	3.6
NHS	3.0	3.3	3.7
Defence	1.0	−2.6	−1.7
Social Security	2.8	5.2	0.9

* 1997–8 to 2000–1

There has been a modest acceleration in the growth of expenditure on education and the NHS under New Labour. But the rates of increase in Labour's four years in office have only been between 1.5 and 2 per cent a year higher than the assumed average increase in pay across the economy as a whole (i.e. the levels of expenditure needed to maintain constant staffing levels); so there has been very little scope for improving the service. The effects of this acceleration on total public spending have been partly offset by falls in defence expenditure (though not as fast as in the Major years) and a slower rate of increase in social security expenditure as unemployment has declined. But in the longer run, if public services are to show any marked improvement, we must face the fact that taxation will have to *rise* as a proportion of national income.

The alternative is to encourage increasing numbers of people to turn to private education and health insurance to achieve the standards of service they seek, leaving the rest of the community to make do with second-rate services. This would seem the natural line for the political right to take, with tax breaks for those using the private sector, like the former tax allowances for private health insurance premiums. Indeed, a leading right-wing expert on health economics, Michael Goldsmith, has proposed that all those earning over £35,000 a year should be excluded from the NHS and compelled to rely on private medical insurance.[19] Such an approach is bound to lead to a second-rate service for the rest of the community. For the left, however, the provision of high standards in state education and the NHS should be a fundamental part of their policies. But this would require a more radical approach to taxation.

Taxation

Nobody likes paying taxes, and their unwillingness to do so is enhanced if they think the Government is wasting their money, or that the service is not worth paying for. New Labour have inherited, and accepted, a climate of opinion based on the assumption that anything done by the state is inherently inefficient and would be done better by the private sector – hence privatization and the PPP. Efforts to improve the public services can actually make matters seem worse, if they involve a barrage of destructive criticism of the way schools or hospitals are run today. The former Chief Inspector of Schools, Chris Woodhead, was a major offender in this respect – as was the Prime Minister's spokesman's reference to 'bog-standard comprehensive schools'. Again, it is foolish for ministers to keep saying that the problems in these fields will not be solved by 'throwing money at them', when the improvements needed will not take place without the money to attract and employ more teachers and medical staff.

How then should a government determined to improve public services tackle the problem of financing them? The Fabian Society Commission on Taxation and Citizenship, which reported in 2000,[20] suggested that one essential was to make the public feel a greater 'connection' between the taxes they pay and the services they get. The most obvious way is to 'hypothecate', or earmark, the revenue for certain taxes to certain services. They acknowledge the difficulties of doing this on any widespread scale, because of the fact that the expenditure required on a particular service and the revenue from a particular earmarked tax might move in different ways. But they proposed splitting the present income tax in two with one part becoming a hypothecated NHS tax. (This would be a modern version of the original 'health stamp' that employees had to put on employees' national insurance cards each week.) Social insurance contributions still represent a hypothecated tax, but given Gordon Brown's objective of integrating the tax and benefit systems, their future is uncertain. The possibilities of some degree of tax earmarking for the state provision of education, health and pensions deserves further consideration.

The ability to raise tax levels depends partly on public attitudes towards the distribution of incomes. The growing inequality of pre-tax income would seem a good justification for making the tax system more progressive, the most obvious candidates being to increase the higher rate of income tax and the effective rate of inheritance tax. It seems ironic to proliferate means-tested benefits with withdrawal rates of 60 per cent or more in order to keep the rate of income tax on the better off down to 40 per cent. The Fabian Commission's recommendation that the higher rate of tax should rise to 50 per cent would command widespread support.

It is time to rethink the philosophy and practice of inheritance taxes. There are strong grounds for using taxation to reduce the growing disparities of inherited wealth, although at the present time the feeling that people should be able to pass on 'their hard-won savings' to their family is increasingly prevalent. This is particularly strongly felt in the case of personal wealth in the form of houses – as is evident in discussion as to how far the state should be financially responsible for long-term care for the elderly. At higher levels of wealth, there are practical problems arising from the ability of the rich to protect and pass on their capital by the use of trusts and other devices.

One of the key facts that rarely enters into the discussion is that most people die and pass on their estate when their children are already well past the stage of buying their first house and struggling to support a young family. It is then their grandchildren who really need financial support. Is there not a case for reviewing the operation of such a tax and relating it to the position of the individuals who receive an inheritance? Inheritance tax could then be combined with a tax on gifts, which would help to combat avoidance. The Fabian Commission advocated a Capital Receipts Tax levied at a progressive rate on the value of gifts and legacies received over an individual's lifetime. There would need to be substantial exemption limits so that members of families could give each other reasonable help in times of difficulty or start the younger members on the housing ladder. But it would be more logical to tax the recipients

48

than the estate as such – although there could still be a small residual levy on the estate as a whole.

Another avenue for relating taxes more closely to the services provided is to give more discretion to devolved bodies, such as the Scottish and Welsh parliaments, and local authorities. There is a good case for allowing local authorities to vary business rates (as they did before the introduction of the council tax) subject to some formula relating the rates of council tax and business rates to avoid excessive reliance on the latter.

It is essential to alter the terms of political debate to recognize that higher living standards mean spending a higher proportion of national income on key public services, and that means a higher proportion of incomes going in taxes. The UK has much the lowest level of government spending in proportion to GDP in the European Union, apart from Ireland. The question we should be asking is: what are the fairest and most acceptable ways of raising the extra money? The Labour Party made a fundamental error by pre-judging the issue and going into the election with a pledge not to raise the basic and higher rates of income tax.

Notes

1. Goodman, A., Johnson, P. and Webb, S., *Inequality in the UK* (Oxford University Press, 1997).
2. National Statistics, *Social Trends* (Stationery Office, 2001).
3. *Social Trends*.
4. Young, M., *Rise of the Meritocracy* (Thames and Hudson, 1959).
5. Tawney, R.H., *Equality* (George Allen and Unwin, 1931).
6. Pimlott, B. (ed.), *Fabian Essays in Socialist Thought* (Heinemann, 1984).
7. Rawls, J., *A Theory of Justice* (Oxford University Press, 1972).
8. Sawyer, M., and O'Donnell, K., *A Future for Public Ownership* (Lawrence and Wishart, 1999).
9. Beveridge, W.H., *Full Employment in a Free Society* (George Allen and Unwin, 1944).
10. Wilkinson, F., *Inflation and Employment: Is there a Third Way?* (Cambridge Journal of Economics, November 2000).
11. See Grieve Smith, J., *Business Strategy*, Chapter 2 (Blackwell, 1990).
12. Marquand, D., *The Unprincipled Society* (Fontana, 1988); Hutton, W., *The State We're In* (Cape, 1995).
13. Dore, R., *Stock Market Capitalism: Welfare Capitalism – Japan and Germany versus the Anglo-Saxons* (Oxford University Press, 2000).
14. *Report of the Commission on Industrial Democracy* (Cmnd 6706, 1977).
15. British Steel Corporation Employee Directors with John Bank and Ken Jones, *Worker Directors Speak* (Gower, 1977).
16. The *Financial Times*, 19 February 2001.

17. *Public-Private Partnerships: The Government's Approach* (HMSO, 2000).
18. *The IFS Green Budget* (January 2001).
19. The *Observer*, 25 February 2001.
20. *Paying For Progress: A New Politics of Tax for Public Spending* (Fabian Society, 2000).

Chapter 3

THE WELFARE STATE

*There are some to whom pursuit of security appears to be a wrong
aim. They think of security as something inconsistent with
initiative, adventure, personal responsibility.*

William Beveridge

1. THE GROWTH OF MEANS-TESTING

Despite the wide-ranging series of changes in social security that the
New Labour government introduced in its first term, the area of so-
called 'welfare reform' is perhaps the one in which their policies are
most clearly dominated by the Thatcherite consensus. After two decades of attacking Tory governments' increasing reliance on means test
ing, New Labour itself has moved further and further down the same
road. One in two pensioners will soon be eligible for means-tested benefits, and well over a million working families. Although increases in the
basic state pension and minimum income guarantee, together with the
proposed pensions credit, will give welcome help to pensioners in the
short run, in the longer run the insistence on continuing to link pensions
and other benefits to prices, rather than earnings, will make them an
increasingly inadequate substitute for lost earnings when people retire,
or are unemployed or sick. We are now at a cross-roads where a basic
political decision has to be made: whether to restore and update the initial
post-war policy of relying primarily on contributory or universal benefits,
or to continue the shift towards means-testing, with the inevitable implication that other benefits will be eventually phased out altogether.

New Labour's welfare reform proposals have been dominated by the
desire to keep down expenditure on benefits and avoid any increase in
income tax. It has been a Treasury-driven exercise throughout. Amid the
welter of glossy documents, there has been no attempt to set out a consistent overall picture of the social security system when the 'reforms' are

51

completed, together with their cost and how they would be financed. This is in stark contrast, for example, to the Beveridge Report, which set out its comprehensive proposals in some detail, including the proposed benefit and contribution rates together with estimates of the total cost and the cost to the Exchequer. One reason for not doing so today is that any longer-term projections with benefits indexed to prices would show a continual rise in the numbers of people dependent on means-tested benefits and their increasing share of the total cost. The Government's tactics appear to be to argue at any one time in favour of targeting any extra money on the poor, but to avoid any discussion of the long-term future of universal benefits – although there can now be little doubt that their implicit strategy is eventually to go over to a completely means-tested system.

The shift in emphasis towards means-testing in recent decades has had the effect of doubling the proportion of benefit income which is means-tested from 16 per cent in 1979 to 32 per cent today.[1] How has this come about? The attraction of increased reliance on means-testing is that it enables any given minimum level of benefit for the poor, for example the Minimum Income Guarantee for pensioners, to be established at a lower cost than if all pensioners got the same benefit. The superficially attractive argument is that 'targeting' expenditure on the least well-off does more to combat poverty than spreading the same amount of money evenly across all pensioners, whatever their income. Why raise state pensions, say Ministers, and give everybody more money, including those already well off? (They never mention the fact that the better-off will be paying 40 per cent income tax on what they receive.) This approach may seem reasonable on the surface but if continued for any length of time, it leads inevitably to the question: why not means-test all benefits? What is the point of maintaining universal benefits? We need to go back to basic principles and examine why the post-war social security system set up a benefit system which was intended to minimize the need for means-testing, and whether the arguments which then prevailed are still valid.

What's wrong with means-testing?

The first major disadvantage of means-tested benefits is in many cases the indignity and feelings of second-class citizenship which come with being subject to severe interrogation and scrutiny by those in authority before receiving any benefits. Such conditional benefits are then bestowed as a 'hand-out', with the implication that the recipient should have been able to do better for himself – that he or she is in effect a member of the 'undeserving poor' or 'underclass'. Moreover, the network of means-tested benefits is becoming increasingly complicated, so that the ordinary citizen cannot possibly be aware of what amount of benefits, if any, he or she is entitled to. Were it not for the help given by Citizens' Advice Bureaux and other voluntary agencies, potential beneficiaries would be totally at the mercy of officialdom. It is not surprising that so many pensioners fail to apply for the benefits to which they are entitled. Up to 700,000 pensioners entitled to income support are not claiming these benefits.[2] At least in their case it should be a more or less once-and-for-all procedure. For those who become unemployed or sick, the circumstances are often more complicated and the scrutiny more frequent and severe. Means-tested benefits are also much more costly to administer than universal benefits. Administrative costs amount to 5 per cent of the value of benefits in the case of income support, whereas the corresponding figure for retirement pensions is only 1 per cent.[3]

The other major drawbacks of means-testing stem from its effects on those whose economic circumstances put them, or could put them, marginally above the level at which they would be eligible for such benefits – much of Tony Blair's 'Middle England'. Those who save small amounts of capital or accumulate a small occupational or private pension will receive correspondingly less from the state when they retire and may be little or no better off than those who have saved nothing.

Correspondingly for those at work, the rate at which the various means-tested benefits are reduced as they earn more means that they are subject to the equivalent of an income tax or 'withdrawal rate' which would be regarded as intolerable for those on higher incomes. It is ironic that in order to avoid raising rates of income tax above 40 per cent on the two million or so people who pay the higher rate, nearly one million people at the bottom of the ladder pay effective rates of 'tax' of 60 per cent or more if their earnings increase. Recent changes have reduced the number of low-earning families subject to withdrawal rates of 90 per cent or more from 130,000 to 30,000 by stretching out the income range over which benefits are withdrawn, but at a cost of increasing the total number of people subject to withdrawal rates of 60 per cent or more from 760,000 to 950,000.[4]

Means-tested benefits involve not only strong disincentives for saving, but also an element of second-class citizenship in which people get financial help by the grace and favour of the rest of the community. As means-testing becomes the predominant source of benefits, the more affluent members of society no longer have a stake in the system, and political support for it is eroded. The arguments against relying on means-testing were strongly put in the Report of the Commission on Social Justice set up by John Smith, which concluded that the aim should be 'to reduce dependence on means-tested benefits to the absolute minimum'.

In an effort to make means-testing more acceptable Gordon Brown has been moving towards integrating the tax and benefits systems, for example, by the Inland Revenue managing the Working Families Tax Credit scheme. This has the laudable objective of reducing any stigma involved, and giving those on benefits greater stability by moving where possible from a weekly to an annual basis of assessment. But the prospect of the Inland Revenue becoming increasingly involved in operating welfare systems raises major issues which have not yet been properly discussed. It would certainly signal the end of state social insurance and the beginning of an era in which state benefits were virtually all subject to an income assessment. Creating an integrated tax and benefit system whilst enlarging the scope of means-tested benefits would underline the fact that the state was taking away more of every extra pound earned by low-paid people with families than from even the most highly paid members of the community. We would have a U-shaped pattern of 'tax' rates, starting with very high rates on those with the lowest incomes, with rates then declining as incomes rose, so that those with middle incomes paid the lowest rates of tax; rates would then rise again so that those on higher incomes were subject to higher tax rates (but not as high as those at the bottom of the income scale).

Welfare to Work

Increased reliance on means-testing is allied to an increasingly authoritarian streak in government policy which seeks to dictate to those on benefit: for example, effectively suggesting that all lone mothers should be at work and leave their children, however young, to be looked after by someone else. New Labour's authoritarian attitude to welfare is most evident in its approach to unemployment. Its policies tend to be based on the assumption that unemployment is due to people being unable or unwilling to take the job available – rather than to a shortage of jobs or inadequate demand for labour. This is in sharp conflict with the facts: post-war experience shows quite clearly that unemployment is primarily determined by the strength of demand for labour. The pattern of regional unemployment makes the same point. People in the areas of high unemployment are not more reluctant to work than people elsewhere: they are victims of a job shortage.

During the first 25 years or so after World War II, when demand was high and unemployment low, 'cash hand-outs' did not lead to 'dependency', despite a benefit regime which New Labour now rejects. The subsequent rise in the number of people on unemployment, sickness and disability benefits was a direct consequence of the oil crisis in the 1970s leading to the Thatcher regime's policy of fighting inflation and breaking the power of the unions by deflationary measures and a steep rise in unemployment. Even though the demand for labour partially recovered in the late 1980s and 1990s, it has not yet regained earlier post-war levels. The fall in unemployment in New Labour's first three years of office was a consequence of an uncovenanted upswing in demand, rather than any of the New Deals or Working Family Tax Credit. Experience shows that when more jobs are available, people take them. The irony is that the movement in demand – the key element in Labour's economic success – was something that they had deliberately placed outside the government's control by giving the Bank of England a free hand in determining monetary policy, and explicitly stating that the Treasury would not use budgetary policy to regulate demand. This has not inhibited ministers from claiming credit for the reduction in unemployment – as, of course, do American presidents who are in a similar position!

Measures to improve training and education for those out of work are important, but they are of little use unless there are sufficient jobs available. Similarly it may be desirable to reduce the positive disincentive to work when people stand to lose a high proportion of the various benefits which they are drawing as they begin to earn wages. But it should be remembered that in the postwar years when the unemployed automatically lost *all* their benefit when they got a job, it was not suggested that people were unemployed because they preferred to be on the dole. Any reasonable benefit system should be predicated on the assumption that people want to work rather than be unemployed. After all, unemployment benefit has always been subject to the condition that people are genuinely seeking work.

Clem Attlee wrote in 1937: 'I can well remember the times when it was assumed that everyone unemployed was so through his own fault... Today unemployment is realized to be in the majority of cases a misfortune due to the maladjustment of the economic machine instead of a failure of character.'[5] It is strange that a Labour government should now turn back the clock and go out of its way to encourage the belief that the unemployed are unwilling to work. It is sad that they, of all people, should revert to a Poor Law mentality and repeatedly suggest that the unemployed are effectively there through their own fault and must be brow-beaten or coerced back into a job. Whoever expected to see Labour ministers' speeches being reported under headlines such as 'Brown tells unemployed "Go get a job"'[6], 'Wake-up call for workshy'[7] and 'No hiding place for fraudsters'.[8] It is not something that families whose lives have been blighted by unemployment will easily forgive. Ministers' constant references to rooting out 'fraud' display a similar cast of mind, suggesting that many of the unemployed are just idle layabouts. Of course, there are some people who cheat the system, just as there are some company directors who fiddle their expenses. But we have yet to hear any minister take a similar stance with the higher echelons of management.

2. NEW LABOUR'S INHERITANCE

The Victorian concept of pauperism, and the undeserving poor was epitomized in the New Poor Law of 1834 which:

> rested upon the assumption that destitution was due to personal failing. It followed that destitution should always be relieved in a way which would encourage self-reliance on the part of the pauper and deter others from seeking relief. In short, poor relief

should be so unpleasant and so degrading that people would turn to their families for support, or, if they were able-bodied, take the work which it was assumed was available.[9]

Although the degrading features of the poor law and the workhouse were ameliorated in the twentieth century, means-testing still aroused bitter resentment. This was most acute in the 1930s when the rising cost of unemployment benefit led the National Government to restrict entitlement to unemployment insurance benefits and made large numbers of the unemployed dependent on means-tested relief from the local Public Assistance Committees (which had taken over the administration of the Poor Law in 1929). The unpopularity of the Household Means Test to which they were subjected was a major factor in the widespread support for the system of mainly contributory benefits proposed in the 1942 Beveridge Report *Social Insurance and Allied Services*, which laid the foundations for the post-war system of social security.

The Beveridge Report

The Beveridge Report reflected the wartime atmosphere of solidarity of the British people and the ideal of common citizenship. This was apparent not only in its objective of minimizing the need for means-testing but also in the proposals for flat-rate benefits paid for by flat-rate contributions (irrespective of an individual's earnings) from both employees and employers. But although contributions were to be levied at a flat rate, the fact that the remaining 50 per cent of the cost was to be paid for by the Exchequer[10] meant that there was an element of redistribution in the scheme, as the burden of taxation fell more heavily on the rich than the poor. The benefits were to be set at the minimum level adequate for subsistence. These would be supplemented by National Assistance, which was intended to cover a much more limited field than the existing means-tested facilities – mainly people who had not made the necessary qualifying contributions, who failed to fulfil conditions for benefit or who had abnormal needs. The Beveridge Committee considered the perennial problem of how to deal with the varying level of rents paid by applicants in different localities but settled for a uniform notional rent component in the universal nationwide level of benefits. An integral part of the Beveridge approach was the introduction of family allowances for children irrespective of whether the parents were drawing benefits or not. One powerful argument for this approach was that if children's allowances were paid only to those drawing benefits, it would increase the potential problem of people suffering a drop in income if they found work.

Under the Beveridge proposals, single working women were treated the same as single men for unemployment benefit and pension purposes. But married working women would receive a lower rate of benefit on the assumption that they were dependent on their husbands. Correspondingly married men on benefit received an additional allowance for dependent (non-working) wives. Two major social changes in the intervening years have been the rise in employment among married women and in the number of unmarried couples. Men and women are now formally treated in the same way; but the fact that someone with a broken contribution record may not qualify for a full pension hits women more than men.

The Beveridge Report illustrated the fact that concern over the effects on the pension bill of people living longer is nothing new. It drew attention to the forecast rise in the number of men over 65 and women over 60 from 12 per cent of the population in 1941 to 17 per cent in 1961. But this was not taken as a reason to curtail the provision of what were regarded as adequate pensions. Beveridge's comments on these projections are, if anything, even more appropriate today. The Report said:

> There is no reason...to doubt the power of large numbers of people to go on working with advantage to the community and happiness to themselves after reaching the minimum pensionable age... The natural presumption for the increasing length of total life is that the length of years during which working capacity lasts will also rise... A people ageing in years need not be old in spirit.[11]

Beveridge distinguished social insurance, organized by the state, from voluntary or private insurance by the fact that membership was compulsory and risks were pooled across the nation: 'each individual should stand in on the same terms; none should claim to pay less because he is healthier or has more regular employment.' One of the questions we have to ask in reviewing the future of social insurance today is how far increasing reliance on private insurance is putting the vulnerable at greater risk. New developments in gene testing may precipitate fresh thinking on this issue. If those of us most likely to be healthy or ill, or live longer or shorter lives, can be identified by insurers, a new era of private insurance will open up, with companies charging differential rates for life insurance, annuities and health insurance to different groups, and in some cases not being prepared to insure people at all. This would very quickly bring the concept of social insurance back into prominence.

Post-war legislation

The 1946 National Insurance Act embodied the basic principles of the Beveridge Report. As far as pensioners were concerned, it was, however, more generous in that the new pension rates came into effect from the start, rather than after a transition period. In the same year universal family allowances were introduced. This was followed by the 1948 National Assistance Act, which set up the National Assistance Board to provide additional, means-tested help for those in need. The number of people on national assistance rose from a million at the end of 1948 to just under 1.8 million by the end of 1954, and stood at around two million when the Board was abolished in 1966.[12]

The initial post-war system remained virtually unchanged for the best part of 30 years. The first change of principle was the introduction of earnings-related supplements to pensions in 1961 and at the same time a move from flat rate to graduated contributions. This was the first step along the road to SERPS: the State Earnings-Related Pension Scheme set up in 1976, 20 years after the Crossman Plan first proposed that the state should offer a universal alternative to employer-run occupational pension schemes. A further step along the road to relating benefits to previous earnings came in 1966 when earnings-related supplements became payable for the first six months of entitlement to unemployment and sickness benefit. The move towards earnings-related benefits, however, fell a victim to the changing political and economic atmosphere of the 1980s.

The Conservative reaction

The Thatcherite desire to cut back the role of the state coincided with increasing expenditure on benefits as unemployment rose to levels unprecedented since World War II. Unemployment doubled between 1979 and 1981, reaching three million in 1982 and remaining there until 1987. The desire to reduce expenditure led to both an extension of means-testing and a retreat from earnings-related benefits. What was then a distinctive Tory attitude was a major theme in Tony Barber's 1970 Budget when he said: 'We intend to adopt a more selective approach to the social services... Instead of the present indiscriminate subsides, help will go where it is most needed' – a theme reiterated by Alistair Darling today. In the same year Keith Joseph introduced the Family Income Supplement, a means-tested benefit designed to help those with children without having to raise the general level of family allowances or extend them to the first child. The supplement was reduced by 50p for every £1 of earnings above the maximum qualifying level. In addition wage earners would begin paying income tax and social insurance contributions, increasing the effective withdrawal rate to 85 per cent. They could also lose rate and rent rebates. This sparked off intensified discussion of the so-called 'poverty trap'.

The Family Income Supplement (FIS) was not quite the first scheme to break new ground in subsidizing low wages. The Labour Government had gone a small step down this road in introducing rate and rent rebates in 1967. Previously benefits had either been directed at those not in work or had been paid irrespective of income, like family allowances. But the FIS set successive governments more firmly on this path, culminating in New Labour's scheme for Working Families Tax Credits.

A further watershed in the history of post-war social security provision was the decision in Geoffrey Howe's first Budget in 1979 to break the link which had been effectively established between benefits and earnings, and instead uprate benefits only with price increases. In the immediate post-war years of low inflation, benefits were neither linked to prices nor earnings, but were up-rated on an *ad hoc* basis. Between 1948 and 1964 insurance benefits were raised six times and means-tested benefits ten times.[13] But the 1974 Labour government announced that it would index pensions and long-term benefits for the sick and disabled to increases in earnings or prices, whichever was the greater – while unemployment and short-term sickness benefit would only be up-rated with prices. The subsequent abolition of the earnings link started a process of whittling away the value of pensions and other benefits in relation to the earnings they were replacing. The basic state pension was equivalent to around 20 per cent of average earnings in the early 1980s, but is now worth only 15 per cent of average earnings and if it continues to be indexed to prices will only be worth 7 per cent of average earnings by 2050.[14]

The overriding objective of the Thatcher government's social (and other) policies in the 1980s was to reduce the cost of benefits and cut taxes on income. Targeting benefits on the poor and indexing benefits only to prices was one way of doing this. Encouraging private provision of pensions by the introduction of the Personal Pension Scheme in 1988 and the downgrading of SERPS was another. New Labour has gone one step further, replacing SERPS with a State Second Pension Scheme. This will initially be a transition measure, but (if still in existence) will eventually become a second flat-rate pension indexed to prices for those in a particular income bracket, and which people can contract out of.

3. WELFARE REFORM

Despite its criticism while in opposition, New Labour has adopted virtually the same philosophy as its Conservative predecessors, whilst taking a more generous view of the level of means-tested benefits which should be available to the least well-off. In the case of pensions, they have introduced the more generous minimum income guarantee to replace the former income support scheme, but have notably failed to index the basic state pension to earnings. The Government has also consolidated Conservative means-tested benefits for helping families with low incomes by introducing the Working Families Tax Credit to replace the Family Credit introduced by Norman Fowler in 1984.

Tax credits

The WFTC is implicitly based on two highly debatable assumptions. The first is that it is preferable to help working families by means-tested benefits rather than by raising universal child benefits. The second is that the government should be prepared to subsidize low wages to increase employment. The alternative to the WFTC would be to raise child benefit. When Family Allowances (as they were then called) were first introduced at the end of World War II, the cost of bringing up children was seen as the extra cost of providing accommodation, food and clothing. Today, the major part of the cost is the loss of earnings if one of the parents stays at home to look after the children, or the cost of child-care if they do not. In either case, the level of Child Benefit does not attempt to cover this. We should be considering tackling this problem in two ways. The first is the Government paying a substantially higher level of (taxable) benefit to all parents, with a higher rate for children of pre-school age, leaving parents a free choice as to whether they go out to work or look after their children themselves. An enhanced, universal child benefit would not only be a major weapon in the fight to reduce family poverty, but would also improve the balance between those with children and those without at all levels of income. In addition the Government should review the cost and extent of childcare provision by local authorities, in all forms: pre- and after-school clubs, playgroups and nursery classes and holiday activities.

A special factor in the rise in poverty among children has been the increase in the number of single parents. Since 1979 the percentage of children in households with only one parent has doubled, and nearly two-thirds of children of single parents are in poverty. This reflects the fact that most lone parents are either not working or are in badly paid jobs: but even where lone parents are working, their income is on average only equivalent to three-fifths of that of couples with children. The Government is trying to assist low-income families by the introduction of the Child Care Tax Credit for those who go out to work. But this seems fundamentally misconceived. Lone parents taking part in a recent piece of research commissioned by the DSS commented that:

they were unhappy 'passing over' their children to a registered carer they did not know. This was especially the case for those who received help from their family or friends with childcare. For them it was a shortcoming that payment could not go to someone who knew their children and whom they trusted.[15]

Why should the state help with the cost of paying strangers to look after children, but not their mothers or other members of the family? Higher child benefits and improved childcare facilities would be a better alternative.

The second debatable assumption is that it is preferable to subsidize low wages rather than to set the minimum wage at an adequate level – a prime example being the Government's proposal to introduce an 'employment tax credit' for single people and couples without children from 2003. This approach reflects the belief that as employment increases, the level of wages that employers can afford to pay additional workers goes down because unit costs rise as output increases – and hence if the marginal workers are to get jobs their pay must be kept down. This tacit assumption (in economic jargon, the doctrine of 'decreasing returns') is one of the commonest fallacies in contemporary economics. As every manager knows, in most fields of industrial activity, the reverse is true – costs per unit decline as output increases. This is because overheads or fixed costs remain broadly the same, and the output per head of the additional workers is similar to that of the existing labour force. This is true in a typical factory or in service trades, like hotels. The fact that the marginal workers may be less experienced, or in some way less competent, is generally of much less significance. Provided the demand for their output is increasing, it generally pays employers to take on more staff on at least the current level of pay. It was sensible to set the minimum wage at a relatively low level to start with to avoid starting a new spiral of wage demands; but as time goes by it should be gradually increased to a higher level, and then kept in line with the rise in average wages. Such increases should not be regarded as an impediment to reducing unemployment: there is clear evidence that the introduction of the minimum wage has had no such effect.[16]

The Treasury estimates that nearly 400,000 of the 1.5 million families who should be eligible for WFTC are not actually claiming it.[17] Rather than putting more working families on means-tested benefits, and hence making them subject to higher marginal rates of what is effectively income tax, the best way of tackling family poverty would be to raise child benefits, improve the availability of childcare facilities and raise the minimum wage. The minimum wage should be set at a level which makes it unnecessary to subsidize recipients without children by such devices as the proposed employment tax credit.

Pensions

Pensions, which account for by far the largest part of expenditure on benefits, are the main field in which the general public has become aware of the shift towards means-testing. Ministers have emphasized the virtues of targeting and taken the line that it does not matter whether benefits are universal or means-tested – it is how much the poor get that counts. Alistair Darling, the Secretary of State for Social Security, made this claim in his evidence to the House of Commons Social Security Committee during its inquiry into the Contributory Principle: 'We believe that the welfare state needs to be focused on outcomes rather than on the means of delivery... If you increase the basic state pension by what-ever amount you want, it does not help the poorest pensioners...' But people who have paid their social security contributions and taxes all their working lives expect a decent pension as of right, not as a form of state charity after an orgy of form-filling and cross-examination. It is no wonder that nearly three-quarters of a million pensioners do not claim the benefits to which they are entitled. If targeting is the criterion, a rise in the basic pension to the level of the Minimum Income Guarantee would be the most effective way of making sure that all pensioners in poverty get the benefits they need.

To qualify for the new Minimum Income Guarantee from April 2001 pensioners must have savings of less than £12,000, and to qualify for the full support, savings of less than £6,000. This creates understandable resentment, and reduces the incentive to make provision for one's old age. To mitigate this, Gordon Brown has put forward proposals for a new Pension Credit to ease the problem of those with relatively small amounts of capital or low second pensions; but however complex the provisions, this difficulty will not go away as long as the basic pension remains below the level of means-tested benefit.

Under the Pension Credit Scheme to come into effect in 2003, the minimum income guarantee would only take into account *income* from savings and not *capital*. The Minimum Income Guarantee means test would be adjusted so that pensioners with small incomes from saving would get 60p more than at present for every £1 of their savings incomes, up to a maximum of £12 for a savings income of £20 a week.[18] Thus someone with £20 a week savings income would get £15 a week from the Minimum Income Guarantee (on top of the basic pension of £77) instead of £3 under the present rules. This would, however, only leave a person with a savings income of £20 a week £12 better off than someone who had no such income. Then for every extra £1 savings income over £20 a week the amount received from the MIG would decline by 40p in the pound until pensioners received nothing extra when their savings income reached the comparatively low maximum of £60 a week. Thus while the Pension Credit would make the Minimum Income Guarantee a little more generous for those with a restricted band of savings incomes, it would involve what is in effect a tax rate of 40 per cent on low occupational pensions and income from savings; and would mean that half of pensioner households would face a means test. In addition many pensioners would also receive less Housing benefit or Council Tax Benefit if their savings income were higher. Taking into account these two benefits as well as the Minimum Income Guarantee, the Institute of Fiscal Studies estimate that under the rules in force at the time of the pre-election budget, 1.8 million pensioners would stand to lose over 80 per cent of any extra savings income in lower benefits.[19]

Raising the basic pension

Reducing the dependence of pensioners on means-tested benefits is partly a matter of increasing the basic state pension, but it also raises two other issues. One is the treatment of people who do not qualify for a full pension because they have not paid enough contributions. The other (closely related) point is the position of married women who are at present getting only a dependant's allowance on the basis of their husbands' contributions – an allowance which assumes (realistically) that a couple can live more cheaply than two single people. As Holly Sutherland has proposed, one way of dealing with these two issues is to make everyone over retirement age entitled to a Citizen's Pension at the same rate for men and women irrespective of their work and contribution record.[20] Abolishing present contribution conditions would solve the problem of carers and parents staying at home to look after their children – but at the expense of weakening people's feeling that they had explicitly contributed to their state pension. This might be alleviated if the concept of crediting people with contributions were extended to cover all forms of 'caring', i.e. looking after children, the disabled or older people; however, there would be a large grey area of people tempted to say that they were 'caring' for an elderly relative, although in practice they did not do much about it. Again, it is arguable whether couples sharing a house need as high a pension as two individuals living on their own, but as increasing numbers of retired couples will not in future be officially married, treating people purely as individuals irrespective of whether they are living together may be a practical necessity. The proposed simple Citizen's Pension may therefore be the most practical solution in the end.

Introducing the proposed Citizen's Pension at the same level as the state pension for single people (£64.70 a week) would have cost an estimated £2.2 billion per annum in 1998 – less than 3 per cent of the total benefit bill. A more generous scheme with a Citizen's Pension of £90 a week (i.e. £25.30 more than then basic pension) would have cost around £10 billion or 1.3 per cent of GDP; and would reduce the number of pensioners on income support by 80 per cent.[21] This could be financed in a number of ways. If it were done solely by raising NI contributions, this would require an increase of 4.6 per cent. This would, however, be reduced if the opportunity were taken to abolish altogether the anomalous upper earnings limit above which income increases incur no additional contributions. If the cost were financed solely by increasing income tax it would require an increase of less than 1 per cent in the standard and lower rates, if the top rate were increased to 50 per cent. The cost of raising the basic pension in this way would depend, of course, on its level at the time. In 2001–2 the basic state pension (for single pensioners) is £72.50 a week and the minimum income guarantee £92.15 – a gap of just under £20, rather less than in Sutherland's estimates. The cost of putting the basic pension up to the minimum guarantee level could therefore be rather less.

These figures suggest that the short-term cost of a shift away from means-tested benefits for pensioners should be within the limits of political acceptability, once we can get away from the present Dutch auction to reduce tax rates. The fundamental reform needed is to set the basic state pension at the same level as the minimum income guarantee. Since revenue from contributions and taxation can also be expected to increase broadly in line with earnings or national income, such a shift would not present a longer term financial problem, were it not for the concern about the forecast increase in the ratio of pensioners to workers – the so-called 'ageing time bomb'. Although these demographic projections are concerned with the situation 10, 20 or 30 years ahead, they have affected the treatment of pensioners today and have been a largely unstated rationale of the Government's failure to relate state pensions to earnings and its increasing reliance on means-tested benefits. It is time they were considered more critically.

4. THE DEMOGRAPHIC TIME BOMB

Official comparisons of the long-term costs of indexing pensions to prices or earnings are based on population projections (which are notoriously subject to error) by the Government Actuary's Department.[22] These projections suggest that the number of people over the state pension age in Great Britain will rise from 10.5 million in 1999 to 13.8 million in 2030, despite the increase in the pension age for women from 60 to 65. Although there is expected to be an increase in the population of working age from 35.5 million to 36.7 million over the same 30-year period, this is relatively small proportionately, so that the ratio of the number of people of working age to those of pension age is expected to fall from 3.4 to 2.7.

The forecast rise in the number of pensioners by 2030 (including those living overseas) is somewhat greater, from 10.9 million to 15.2 million, reflecting the number of women who qualified for pension before the pension age reached 65. (It is due to be phased up from 60 to 65 between 2010 and 2020). In parallel, the Government Actuary's Department estimates that the ratio of the number of people contributing to the National Insurance Fund to the number of pensioners would fall from 1.8 to 1.4

Despite the growing number of pensioners, the Government Actuary's Department has estimated that the cost of indexing the basic state pension to earnings from 2003 (and taking into account the increases proposed in the Pre-Budget Report for the next two years) could be met by running down the accumulated surplus in the National Insurance Fund up to 2006–7 without increasing the rate of NI contributions required.[23] In the longer run, however, the joint NI contribution rate (employers and employees) would have to rise to 27 per cent in 2030 from today's level of 20 per cent; whereas if pensions were only linked to prices the contribution rate could come down to 19 per cent.

The cost of the basic state pension in 2030–31 (in 2000 prices) would be £49 billion if the pension were linked to prices and £77 billion if linked to earnings – as compared with £34 billion in 2000–1. By 2030–31 the additional cost of indexing pensions to earnings would thus be £28 billion. This comparison, however, does not take into account the corresponding *saving* in spending on means-tested benefits if benefits were indexed to earnings rather than prices. No official estimates of this saving are available – a striking omission if there is to be any reasonable discussion of the alternatives.

It is projections on these lines that have stimulated discussion (both in the UK and elsewhere) of the 'demographic time-bomb' and growing burden of meeting the costs of pensions. But even the most superficial examination of the problem suggests that the vast edifice of calculations based on the projections by the Government's Actuary's Department (and others) of the proportion of the population over 65 does not tell the real story. This depends on the number of people at work relative to those who are in some sense 'dependent' – this would include pensioners, children and people of working age who are not working. Insufficient attention has been paid to the fact that the rise in the number of older people over the next 30 years will be partly offset by the decline in the number of children, which is expected to go down by one million. In real terms the key point is that the consumption of those not at work has to be met from the production of those who are. The crucial assumption in the Government Actuary's Department's professionally conservative estimates is that the numbers at work in

2030 would be 27.2 million or 45.3 per cent of the total population as compared with 27.6 million or 47.8 per cent in 1999. It would therefore need only another 1.5 million people at work to maintain the same ratio of workers to dependents.

Getting more people into work

Examination of the Government Actuary's assumptions about 'activity rates' (i.e. proportion of people in the labour market) at different ages suggests that such an increase is well within the bounds of possibility. The Appendix to this chapter shows the Government Actuary's Department estimates of activity rates in 1999 and 2030 and an alternative estimate for 2030 assuming that by then men and women are working longer. On these alternative assumptions there would be over 1.7 million more people over the age of 55 at work, one million of whom would be women. Health apart, activity rates for older women seem likely to increase appreciably as the higher proportion of younger women now working grow older.

The slackening of demand for labour in the 1980s has left a legacy of low levels of employment among men over 50, particularly in some northern areas dependent on manufacturing industry. More effective policies to get more jobs into the northern areas of the country with heavy unemployment could significantly reduce the cost of uprating benefits and increase the revenue to meet them. The scope for increasing activity rates among older people is illustrated by the fact that in the period March–May 2000 the activity rate for men from 50 to 64 and women from 50 to 59 was only 61.3 per cent in Wales, as against 76.8 per cent in the South East. These figures suggest that any effects of greater prosperity in leading to voluntary early retirement are more than outweighed by the effects of stronger demand in keeping people in jobs. Given a strong demand for labour and a greater willingness to employ older people, it is not difficult to envisage sufficient increase in activity rates to maintain the current ratio of workers to non-workers across the population as a whole, allowing for the expected decrease in the number of children. As health improves and people live longer they will also be capable of, and wish to, work longer.

Such an increase in activity rates would go a long way to offsetting the cost of the growing number of pensioners. It has been estimated that getting another million people into work would save about £3 billion a year in expenditure on unemployment, sickness and disability benefits etc and raise about £7 billion extra in taxes and insurance contributions.[24] The resulting £10 billion a year would meet the cost of benefits for over three million pensioners. Thus getting another 1.5 million older people under pension age into work would broadly pay for the additional cost of benefits for the additional 4.3 million pensioners expected in 2030 (as compared with 1999) at today's level of pensions in relation to earnings. Moreover with improved employment possibilities, there would be fewer pensioners than at present projected as more people over 65 remained in work.

Such estimates suggest that the economic 'burden' of the changing age structure, and hence the need to keep down pensions, is in danger of being considerably over-rated. The key to the 'ageing problem', such as it is, is not to pare down pension support for the retired, but to establish the conditions for greater participation in the labour market by the over-50s. To make this possible, it will be necessary to maintain a high demand for labour, so that as older people come onto the labour market they are additional to, not replacements for, younger people. It will also need a change in attitude by employers and others, including the abolition of compulsory retiring ages and, more controversially, gradual increases in the standard ages of retirement in state and occupational pension schemes, combined with flexible pensions for early and late retirement. If the standard retirement age for calculating pensions is 65 today, it would be reasonable to expect it to be somewhat higher in 20 or 30 years' time.

Second Pensions

The most confusing part of the pension system is the area of state and private 'second' pensions, i.e. pensions additional to the basic state pension. Occupational schemes have generally been the best in this field because they have stable rules linking pensions to earnings, and employers both make a significant contribution to the cost and take the risk of additional contributions being needed because of vagaries in stock market prices or interest rates or the age and pay structure of their employees.

Stakeholding and other personal private pensions are subject to considerable uncertainty over the eventual value. The main drawback to occupational schemes, however, is the difficulty of transferring from one scheme to another – the principal exception being certain parts of the public sector. For salary earners expecting to move up the salary grades during the course of their career, merely being credited with the value of the accrued money contributions when they move is much less valuable than being credited with their number of years' service. It is important therefore to keep such transfer provisions under public review.

The Government's own contribution in this field is to replace SERPS with the curiously conceived Second State Pension. Initially it will be a more generous substitute for the emaciated version of SERPS left after successive Conservative cuts. But eventually it will merely be a second flat-rate pension also indexed to prices, and hence getting progressively less significant in replacing the loss of earnings on retirement. By 2050, the flat-rate second pension will be rather higher than the flat-rate basic pension: £35 per week in terms of today's earnings against £30 per week for the basic pension.[25] This gives a total pension equivalent in present-day terms to £65 per week. So the Government's long-term concept is an increasingly meagre state pension of which people may contract out of over half, i.e. the Second State Pension portion. If they can contract out of part of the flat-rate pension, then the next step will be to permit contracting out of the whole thing.

In an age of growing labour mobility, a straightforward state earnings-related scheme, with its relatively low administrative costs, would seem a valuable alternative to private schemes, such as personal or stakeholding pensions, with the uncertainties inherent in money purchase schemes about future share prices and interest rates. Again, ill-judged panic about future costs seems to be behind the decision to abolish, rather than reform, SERPS. It seems difficult to believe that the proposed Second State Pension will survive for long in its present form, but it has created yet another source of uncertainty about future benefits.

5. TIME TO TAKE STOCK

The current policy debate on social security policy has tended to concentrate on the question of indexing pensions to earnings rather than prices. This is only one facet of the Government's implicit strategy of abandoning the post-war social security system and moving over to a system of means-tested benefits. The introduction of the Employment Credit and Integrated Child Tax Credit will mean that large numbers of people with relatively low earnings will be subject to higher 'withdrawal' (in effect tax) rates on any increases in income than the better paid. The integration of the tax and benefit systems will highlight the anomalous nature of such a system. Under the previous system of universal pensions and child benefit (with means-tested supplements in exceptional cases), the vast majority of people were subject to a truly progressive tax system starting with relatively low rates of tax on low incomes and higher rates moving up the income scale. But under the integrated tax and benefit system now being developed we are moving to a system in which low earners pay high rates of tax on any additional income, those on middle incomes pay low rates and the well-off pay higher rates, but not as high as those on low incomes. It seems difficult to believe that anyone would consciously design such a basically indefensible system *ab initio*. It is time that all the ramifications of this strategic issue was brought out into the open, and the expenditure and taxation implications of re-establishing a new social security system properly assessed.

Notes

1. House of Commons Social Security Committee report on *The Contributory Principle*, June 2000.
2. DSS evidence to House of Commons Social Security Committee, November 1999.
3. *Social Security Departmental Report*, Cm 4614, April 2000.
4. *Budget 2000*, Table 4.2.
5. Attlee, C., *The Condition of the Labour Party* (Gollancz, 1937).
6. *Sunday Times*, 27 February 2000
7. *Daily Mail*, 5 April 2000
8. The *Observer*, 14 January 2001
9. Deacon, A. and Bradshaw, J., *Reserved for the Poor: The Means Test in British Social Policy*, (Blackwell and Robertson, 1983).
10. Beveridge, W., *Social Insurance and Allied Services* (md 6404, 1942): Table XII.

11. Beveridge Report p. 99.
12. Deacon and Bradshaw (op. cit.).
13. Timmins, N., *The Five Giants: A Biography of the Welfare State* (Fontana, 1996).
14. Banks, J. and Emmerson, C., *Public and Private Pension Spending: Principles, Practice and the Need for Reform*, Fiscal Studiesvol. 21, no. 1 (2000).
15. Unemployment Unit *Working Brief*, October 2000.
16. Second Report of the Low Pay Commission, Cm 4571, 2000.
17. Financial Times 24 October 2000; DSS Consultation Paper: *The Pension Credit*, Cm 4900, November 2000.
18. *The Pension Credit*.
19. Clark, T., *Recent Pensions Policy and the Pensions Credit* (Institute of Fiscal Studies, 2000).
20. Sutherland, H., *A Citizen's Pension*, Microsimulation Unit Discussion Paper MU 9804.
21. Sutherland, op.cit.
22. *Quinquennial Review of National Insurance Fund* by the Government Actuary's Department, Cm 4406.
23. *Report by the Government Actuary On the Cost of Uprating The Basic Retirement Pension In Line With The General Level of Earnings*, Cm 4920.
24. These estimates (at 1996/7 price and income levels) are from Kitson, M., Michie, J. and Sutherland, H., *The Fiscal and Distributional Implications of Job Generation* (Cambridge Journal of Economics, January 1997). The cost of state pensions per head in 1996/7 was £3,220 (Cm 4614).
25. DSS, *A Partnership in Pensions*, Cm 4179 (Chart 5), 1998.

APPENDIX

EFFECTS OF CHANGES IN ACTIVITY RATES

1. Activity Rates (per cent)[1]

Age	1999 Actual	Men 2030 GAD forecast	2030 Alternative forecast	1999 Actual	Women 2030 GAD forecast	2030 Alternative forecast
16–19	67.9	62.9		63.1	61.4	
20–24	83.7	85.7		70.5	74.1	
25–34	93.3	91.0		75.2	79.9	
35–44	92.0	89.4		77.0	78.6	
45–54	88.5	87.3		76.8	82.7	
55–59	74.6	71.1	80	53.1	54.5	75
60–64	53.8	49.2	65	30.3	36.0	60
65–69	15.0	13.0	20	3.5	3.8	10
70+	4.6	4.4	7	3.5	3.8	5

2. Extra numbers in labour force in 2030 on alternative assumption (thousands)[2]

	Men	Women
55–59	172	383
60–64	337	504
65–69	144	129
70+	109	65
	762	1081

Total additional active	1843
less 4.7% unemployed (GAD estimate)	87
Total additional employed	1756

Notes

1. The first column (for both men and women) shows activity rates (percentage of people of working age seeking or at work) for 1999, and the second the estimate used by the Government Actuary for 2030 in Table 14.1 in his Quinquennial Review of the National Insurance Fund (Cm 4406, July 1999). The alternative estimate in the third column gives greater weight to the desire of older people to carry on working and to the effects of raising the state pension age for women from 60 to 65 by the year 2020.
2. The difference between the two activity rates for 2030 has been multiplied by the Government Actuary's population forecasts by age group for 2030 in Table 13.1 of the Quinquennial Report.

Chapter 4

THE FUTURE OF THE EU

We must build a kind of United States of Europe.

Winston Churchill (in Zurich), 1946

1. FURTHER INTEGRATION

The economic and political future of the European Union is now dominated by the existence of the Economic and Monetary Union (EMU) and the euro – a striking example of the ascendancy of the New Orthodoxy, making an independent central bank the most powerful economic institution in the Community. Whilst the UK, Denmark, Greece and Sweden remain uncommitted to joining the currency union, new applicants for EU membership (the so-called Accession Countries) are committed in principle to join once they are regarded as fit to do so. There is a curious asymmetry in this. On the one hand, the EU appears to be developing into a two-tier system with the euro countries constituting the federal core. On the other hand, the existing four non-euro members would seem more likely members of the inner circle than most of the Accession Countries. We need to consider the future of the EU either as a single unit in which all countries participate on a similar footing, or for an interim period at any rate, as a more diverse community – either with two tiers, defined according to whether members are in or out of EMU, or a multispeed Union in which different groups of countries co-operate most closely in various fields: for example, the participants in a common defence force might differ from those in EMU. In either event, political and economic integration seems likely to be a continuing process lasting many decades, not something which will suddenly reach an end-point embodied in a final treaty in the next few years.

Moves to closer economic co-operation are closely linked to the development of the political structure. The founding fathers of the community, Jean Monnet and Robert Schuman, always thought of economic union as leading to a political union which would banish for ever the possibility of another Franco-German war, such as they had seen twice in their lifetimes. However, the creation of EMU has meant that political integration is now lagging well behind economic integration. In the past the adoption of a common currency in an area would generally have been associated with the existence of a common government for that area. A distinctive currency was regarded as an attribute of sovereignty and something ultimately under the control of the government of that territory. It is only the neo-liberal revolution in economic thinking in the 1980s that made it possible for the Delors Committee to conceive of a central bank running a European currency without an overarching European government or any form of democratic control.[1] It is ironic that such a situation should become acceptable at the same time as monetary policy has come to be regarded as the sole legitimate means of regulating demand, thus removing the key element in European economic policy, demand management, from democratic control. In addition, although responsibility for exchange rate policy remains nominally with finance ministers, the fact that its execution is essentially a central bank function, and ministers cannot issue directives to the ECB, is another constitutional anomaly.

The future political structure of the EU is closely related to the economic philosophy on which it is based, because this determines the functions of government which need to be undertaken at a European level. We then have to ask what is the most effective democratic machinery for carrying them out. Is it a continuation or development of the existing *intergovernmental* structure supported by the European Commission and scrutinized by the European parliament; or should it be some form of *elected* European government? The original concept of a common market placed the emphasis on the removal of barriers and restrictions to trade within the Community. It followed that the prime functions to be undertaken at a European level were regulatory. The major exception has been the operation of the Common Agricultural Policy, the largest component of the total EU budget, and originally France's *quid pro quo* for giving German industry free access to French markets.

The centralization of certain functions at a European level follows more or less inevitably from the creation of the common market and now

76

the monetary union. International trade policy is an obvious case. But just as the free movement of goods within the EU necessitates a common international trade policy, so the free movement of people must in the end lead to a common immigration policy – at present only partially achieved in the Schengen Agreement, to which the UK has not yet subscribed. Again, effective policies to develop poorer regions with above-average unemployment require the ability at a European level to concentrate more investment on infrastructure in these areas and discriminate in such a way as to give financial incentives for industry to invest there, rather than elsewhere. Hence the creation of the Structural Funds and the introduction of EU-wide rules on state aid to industry are another logical development. As within the UK, so in Europe: merely encouraging every region to develop on its own initiative, without any discrimination between areas in giving aid from the centre, would strengthen still further the attraction of the already prosperous areas rather than improve the relative position of those that lag behind.

2. MANAGING DEMAND

The field in which the EU has notably failed to get to grips with the relative roles of European-wide and national responsibility is that of macro-economic policy or demand management – one which is crucial to Europe's economic prosperity. The present system of demand management by means of a common monetary policy throughout Euroland raises two types of difficulty. The first is that the pressure of demand is likely to vary between countries, so that higher interest rates may be appropriate to curb inflationary pressures in some countries, while there is no need for deflationary measures in others. The second is that with the present degree of financial integration, changes in interest rates may have more effect on demand in some countries than others (e.g. if one country, such as the UK, has a lower proportion of fixed interest mortgages than others). This suggests that budgetary policy should now have an increasing, rather than diminishing, role to play, as the key instrument under national control which can be used to cope with differing demand and conditions in different countries.

Stability and Growth Pact

Governments' freedom to pursue active fiscal policies is, however, heavily circumscribed by the so-called Stability and Growth Pact, finalized in Amsterdam in 1997.[2] It is perverse that this should be directed exclusively towards tightening budgetary policy and eliminating deficits with no provision for the use of fiscal policy as a stimulus. In this, of course, it follows the Maastricht Treaty. The Pact commits countries to a 'medium-term budgetary position of close to balance or in surplus'. If the planned or actual deficit exceeds 3 per cent of GDP, the country is liable to incur a financial penalty imposed by the Council of Ministers. The only automatic exception is when the excessive deficit arises from 'an unusual event outside the control of the Member State concerned' or results from an economic downturn involving an annual fall of real GDP of at least 2 per cent a year. (There is, however, a clause which allows a state to claim a possible exception if the fall in output exceeds 0.75 per cent a year and there has been an accumulated loss of output relative to past trends.) Where the circumstances are not regarded as 'exceptional', the Council can impose a penalty in the form of a non-interest bearing deposit which can be converted into a fine after two years.

The deflationary bias of the Stability and Growth Pact was illustrated early in 2001 by the Commission's pressure on the British and Irish Governments to adopt less expansionary budget plans. In the British case the criticism was directed at a potential deficit in 2005, rather too far ahead to take any view on the appropriate fiscal stance. In the Irish case the criticism was based on the fact that inflation was running above the average EMU level. It was notable that there was no question of pressing countries like Germany and France with heavy unemployment to adopt more expansionary polices.

The Pact virtually rules out the use of fiscal policy to stimulate the European economy when threatened with recession, or to stimulate a faster growth in demand to bring down unemployment. This could become increasingly serious as the threat of world-wide inflation recedes whilst the high level of unemployment remains a major threat to Europe's economic and political stability. The Pact fails to acknowledge the possibility of excessive surpluses. The irony is that the budget deficits that the finance ministers and the Commission were so concerned about were mainly the consequence of a prolonged period of low demand. The one thing that would make European budgets healthier would be a period of faster expansion – something the ECB is anxious to avoid!

An important corollary of the new monetary arrangements associated with the single currency should be a fresh look at the use of national budgetary policies in such a way as to cope with differing conditions in different countries, but also to ensure that the combined fiscal stance for the whole EMU area is appropriate for demand conditions at the time, whether the immediate danger is of inflationary pressure on the one hand, or of heavy or rising unemployment on the other. When Euroland as a whole is facing either marked inflationary or deflationary conditions, there may be a need for co-ordinated fiscal measures to damp down or stimulate demand, rather than leaving it all to monetary policy. This could be particularly important when there is a danger of recession, and lower interest rates on their own may not be sufficiently effective in stimulating demand. Thus fiscal policy 'co-ordination' must have two aims. The first is to ensure that differences in fiscal stance between countries reflect any differences in macro-economic conditions between them: co-ordination does not mean uniformity. The second is to ensure that the combined fiscal stance reflects the combined macro-economic position.

3. TAXES AND PUBLIC EXPENDITURE

Harmonizing taxes

Closely linked to the issue of making more active use of fiscal policy is the question of tax harmonization. How far do taxes need to be harmonized or unified within either EMU, or the EU as a whole, and what are the implications of tax harmonization for fiscal policy? We are entering a new era where there will be a spectrum of taxes ranging from those which can be levied on a purely local basis (such as property taxes) to those that need to be levied at a uniform rate internationally: the prime example of the latter is the proposed (Tobin) tax on foreign currency transactions, followed a close second by taxes on share transactions which will sooner or later have to be levied at a uniform rate worldwide, if transactions are not to become concentrated in tax-free markets. Within this spectrum some taxes need to be harmonized over a region or group of neighbouring countries, whereas others need to be harmonized over a wider area. For example, the present disparity in British and continental rates of tax on alcoholic beverages is too great to continue indefinitely, but there is no suggestion that such harmonization need be extended outside the Common Market (save possibly to close neighbours).

Within large federal states such as the United States, there is room for small differences in sales taxes between component states (i.e. State as opposed to Federal taxes) but such differences need to be limited. When it comes to services, taxes on those that can only be consumed locally (e.g. hairdressing) do not call for harmonization, but those that can be used at a distance (e.g. many financial services) do raise harmonization issues. Again, when it comes to taxes on income, there is room for considerable variation between countries in the rates charged on personal earned income. But when it comes to investment income and the affairs of the mobile rich, differences in national tax rates and the existence of tax havens can frequently be exploited. Similarly, differences in national tax regimes for companies are now affecting the way in which multinationals arrange their affairs. Co-operative action is being taken within the OECD to tackle the problem of tax havens, but the wider issues of harmonization in these fields are only just beginning to come onto the EU agenda, for example, with discussion of possible harmonization of the tax treatment of eurobonds – an issue where the UK government seems to have been deliberately obstructionist in its desire to defend the perceived interest of the City of London. They have had no qualms, however, in imposing the Climate Charge Levy on energy-intensive British manufacturing industries, even though this will merely divert production to their competitors on the continent, or elsewhere, who may be less energy efficient. Our Government and others should be less insular over tax policy and recognize that they will increasingly have to cooperate closely with other governments in this field.

There seems little reason to think, however, that the creation of a common currency in Europe *per se* should significantly affect the issue, save in so far as it leads to generally closer economic co-operation. It is rather the creation of the common market and greater mobility of labour and capital that creates the pressure for harmonization. Thus tax harmonization will remain essentially an EU rather than EMU concern.

Tax harmonization and the need to co-ordinate fiscal policy are both closely linked to the size of the common EU budget. For as the Community develops more common spending programmes (e.g. on a common defence policy), there will be a stronger case for financing them from European taxes rather than levies on individual states. One of the problems of tax harmonization, however, is that once agreement is reached on the rules and rates for levying a particular tax, any changes require discussion and agreement between all the states concerned. This makes them difficult to use as variable elements in any counter-cyclical fiscal policy. The problem of agreeing on common spending policies and tax rates between individual nation states is thus one of the factors that will cause pressure for some form of federal government. It is clearly more practical for a federal finance minister and cabinet to take such decisions than an inter-governmental committee of states. One of the key constitutional problems, however, is that the more states that join the Union, the more difficult it will be to reach inter-governmental decisions, but the less homogeneous will be the potential members of any federal system.

A European Budget

It is strange that so little attention has been paid to the question of a European budget in recent years. This is partly a reflection of the displacement of fiscal by monetary policy as the fashionable means of demand management. The 1977 MacDougall Report[3] examined the practical implications of such a budget (whether it was under inter-governmental or federal control) both for demand management and for redistributing resources within the Community. But now, as then, the total expenditure on such a budget would represent too small a proportion of European GDP to be an effective instrument of demand management. The initial components of an enlarged common budget today would be existing programmes, such as the Common Agricultural and regional policy programmes and the European Defence Force. Another field where closer collaboration could lead to a combined federal and state regime is social security: pensions, unemployment and other benefits. With greater mobility

81

within the Community, social security rights will need to be easily transferable between countries. It would not be practicable to have equal levels of pensions, unemployment benefits etc. in countries as long as there are significantly different levels of real wages; because what might be an adequate replacement for lost earnings in low-income countries would be quite inadequate in other countries with higher standards of living. But there could be a uniform system of *wage-related* unemployment, sickness and retirement benefits and contributions, with differing minimum flat rates of benefit in different countries, based on the average level of wages in each country. This would be consistent with the development of social security provision on the continent where a majority of countries have, for example, state earnings-related pensions schemes[4] – but not, of course, with present British policies, which make no provision for state wage-related pensions or other benefits, and indeed envisage the gradual erosion of flat rate benefits in favour of 'targeting' or means-testing (as discussed in chapter 3).

One feature of earlier discussions about a European budget was its possible beneficial effects in redistributing resources between richer and poorer countries and helping countries which were potentially badly hit by external shocks. Even if expenditure from the budget was evenly spread between countries, financing it by European income or sales taxes would mean that the poorer countries were paying less for the same returns. In so far as expenditure was concentrated in poorer countries to start with (e.g. regional aid) the redistributive effects would be greater. Whatever the level of the European budget, this is a good argument for financing it by means of European taxes rather than by negotiated contributions from national Treasuries, as at present.

The other potential benefit of a European budget would be that if one country were suffering a disproportionate fall in output and employment, for example because of some disturbance in world markets, that country would pay less in European taxes; and, if social security were funded on a European scale, would draw additional benefits. In other words there would be some 'automatic stabilizers' as in the US federal system. But for either of these two stabilizers to have any significant effect, the level of European expenditure and taxation would have to be at a considerably higher level than currently envisaged. To obviate this difficulty and to provide an effective means of helping countries where employment has been particularly badly hit by falling demand, various stabilization schemes have been put forward to give such countries financial assistance from European funds to increase demand there, on either a discretionary or an automatic basis.[5]

4. THE LABOUR MARKET

Wage negotiations

One factor which might lead to unemployment problems in particular parts of EMU is if industrial costs there get out of line, as has happened in the UK car industry. With countries no longer able to adjust their exchange rates, rectifying any such disparities in cost levels is likely to be a slow and painful process. The key to avoiding this problem is to try to ensure that money wages, so far as possible, reflect differences in productivity in different areas.

The growth of pay bargaining on a European scale, in the motor industry, for example, could cause problems in this respect. In so far as there are differences in productivity between one company's plants in, say, Germany and Spain, there is a clear case for preserving differences in wages between areas to reflect this. The difficulty becomes greater, however, if productivity levels in that company or industry, converge whilst substantial differences remain in *average* productivity between countries for their industry as a whole. If the motor industry in Spain pays its workers German-level wages, other firms in the same area are in danger of having to pay wages out of line with their productivity levels and so become uncompetitive. Thus although it may seem unfair to Spanish car workers to be paid less than their German counterparts, the future of their region, and indeed the ability to attract further investment in the car industry there, depends on keeping wages at levels which leave industry *as a whole* in that region competitive with elsewhere. Hence there is a case for what at first sight seems incongruous – emphasis on national or regional, rather than European-wide, wage negotiations. This could be particularly important in the case of new members of Eastern Europe – as the unification of Germany showed, when raising wage rates to Western

German levels in East Germany had disastrous effects on the low productivity industries there. Over the years, with more labour mobility and cross-border investment, productivity levels across Europe will tend to converge, but this will be a slow process. Whilst, however, wage negotiations need to preserve national or regional difference for some time, there is also a need to keep the general rate of increases at a level which will be consistent with acceptably low levels of inflation throughout the EU.

5. A EUROPEAN FEDERATION?

In discussing the future of the EU, most British commentators tacitly assume that what would suit Britain best is necessarily also best for Europe as a whole. That may well not be so. Indeed if the British viewpoint had prevailed, there would not have been a Coal and Steel Community in the first place, nor the subsequent Common Market. Thus the fact that Britain may not want to participate in a European Federation does not obviate the strong case for establishing some form of federal system for those countries which want closer economic and political integration. The constitutional dilemma facing the EU will be that with a possibility of enlargement with up to 27 or more member states, management by inter-governmental co-operation will become increasingly difficult. The choice between continuing with the present inter-governmental approach and some form of federal system rests both on their relative efficiency and on their political acceptability. While a federation would in principle facilitate decision-making, the diversity of the countries concerned could limit the political acceptability of a federal system. On the other hand a federal government with elected cabinet members could be seen as the more democratic option if the media, and hence the electorate, were more focused on political decisions at a European level – and in a more serious way than the present hysterical soundings of the British Eurosceptic press!

The difference between a federal system and the present set-up would be the creation of some form of a democratically elected European government. This might be made up of ministers who were members of the European parliament, by direct presidential election or by a directly elected European cabinet – or, given the Community's constitutional ingenuity to date, some combination of these approaches. Such a 'federation' would have to be based on a constitution under which only specified powers lay with the federal government and all residual powers lay with the individual state. Given the way the EU has evolved, it would probably be wrong to envisage a once-for-all settlement, but rather a minimal list of federal responsibilities to start with, which might be enlarged over the course of time: in other words an initial constitution capable of amendment at reasonable intervals. With such an approach, there would be a continuing need for inter-governmental agreement and co-ordination on matters not within the federal orbit. Thus the supporting bureaucracy would have two roles: (a) to formulate and execute policies which were the responsibility of the federal government, and (b) to service committees of national ministers dealing with particular fields of policy. The European Commissioners would then become in effect heads of departments (Permanent Secretaries in British parlance), but as such would still play a key role in formulating policy.

For many years (at least) it seems probable that Britain will be reluctant to join, in view of our English-speaking, Atlantic and Commonwealth ties. There is a parallel with the position of French-speaking Quebec. Economically it is clearly a part of Canada, but culturally it feels separate. But that should not, and will not, stop others going ahead as they have already done, leaving the UK to decide at a later date whether to participate.

6. RETHINKING EUROPEAN ECONOMIC POLICY

European economic policy is at present still dominated by the New Orthodoxy, which underlay the Treaty of Maastricht and the creation of the single currency. In essence its overriding objective is to limit inflation, and the primary instrument for doing so is monetary policy, in the hands of the European Central Bank. Budgets should be balanced and should not be actively used to regulate demand – though cyclical fluctuations in revenue and expenditure (the *automatic stabilizers*) are acceptable within limits. Unemployment is seen as due to imperfections in the labour market to be met by supply-side measures and deregulation. Ironically, whilst the reduction in unemployment in the UK has been almost entirely due to rising demand, the British government has been trying to thrust supply-side measures and labour market 'flexibility' down the throats of its European colleagues. The tragedy is that the expansion of demand needed in other parts of the EU to reduce the dangerously high level of unemployment there has been ruled out by the European Central Bank's concern solely with inflation, together with national governments' obeisance to the Stability and Growth Pact and their reluctance to use fiscal policy to stimulate demand.

Coordinating policy

It is time for a new start. This will be difficult. The whole concept of an integrated fiscal and monetary demand policy is vitiated by the fact that Article 107 of the Treaty specifically forbids the Council from influencing the European Central Bank in any way. This is particularly serious when the ECB shows little concern for the high rate of unemployment in the euro area. An average level of around 8 per cent conceals concentrations of much heavier unemployment, e.g. in East Germany, which are contributing to the rise in racial violence, and act as a breeding ground for right-wing extremism. Article 103 of the Treaty sets out a procedure for co-ordinating national economic polices. It provides that the Council should draw up broad guidelines for the economic policies of member states and the Community. But an expansionary policy would require some amendment, or reinterpretation, of Article 104 and the Stability and Growth Pact, both of which are outdated cases of 'fighting the last war' in that they tacitly assume that the main danger is one of inflation. The more serious threat to the cohesion of the EU today is its inability to reduce unemployment substantially below 10 per cent – a prerequisite for which is a higher level of demand.

Reducing unemployment will depend on gradually increasing demand faster than the trend rate of growth. The best safeguard against such an expansionary policy leading to inflation lies in the features of the continental wage bargaining systems that Tony Blair and other so-called 'reformers' seem anxious to destroy. 'Flexible' labour markets make it easier to keep down inflation by creating a pool of unemployment, but make it *more* difficult to avoid an inflationary wage/price spiral if demand is expanded to reduce unemployment. If, as they are effectively advocating, wage increases were more dependent on labour market conditions, strengthening the demand for labour would tend to spark off higher wage and price increases. But in so far as wages are subject to collective bargaining on an industry-wide or national scale, there is scope for moderating wage settlements so as to achieve lower unemployment without stimulating faster inflation – this was the key to continental success in earlier post-war years. Obviously in practice there is a mixture of both collective bargaining at a variety of levels and purely market-determined pay. But if the EU is to move nearer to full employment, the need is to follow the Scandinavian pattern and encourage socially conscious, rather than market-determined, wage fixing.

Restoring full employment is not a matter of creating a more 'flexible' and hence volatile labour market, with worse working conditions and less protection for workers. Indeed those who are most anxious for such 'reforms' have no real wish to reduce unemployment and thus increase the economic and political power of the ordinary worker. They prefer the social balance as it is today, rather than as it was in the more egalitarian times of full employment. A truly social-democratic Europe would not be a Blairite paradise but would preserve and enhance the best features of the continental tradition of social partnership.

7. A NEW ERM

The immediate question facing the UK is whether or when we should join EMU. Any considered discussion about whether (or when) the UK should join EMU should examine more closely the policy options for sterling if we stayed outside. At present the tacit assumption is that the choice is either to join, and fix our exchange rate with EMU countries irrevocably, or to carry on with the present policy of allowing sterling to float freely, with all the problems that presents for industry in dealing with our closest trading partners. There is another option (either permanent or transitional) which deserves serious consideration: that is, to establish a managed exchange rate system for the pound and the euro – a new Exchange Rate Mechanism (ERM) – which could include other EU members who had not adopted the euro. The object of such a system would be to maintain the pound at a relatively stable and competitive rate against the euro, but leave room for adjustment as changes in circumstances made this necessary.

Lessons from the past

In setting up a new ERM-style agreement we need, however, to learn from experience and avoid the mistakes of the past. The first, and most obvious, is that the UK, and any other potential members, must join at a realistic exchange rate. Entering the ERM at as high a rate as DM2.95 in October 1990 was a disastrous mistake which precipitated our unseemly exit on Black Wednesday, just under two years later. Given the present excessively high level of sterling, it will be difficult to negotiate a sufficiently low entry rate, but the evident concern of the financial guardians of the euro when it was at a low level should help.

The second lesson is that adjustments in rates should be made in small steps at relatively frequent intervals (rather than waiting for large overdue changes under crisis conditions) as was the case in the early years of the ERM, with some success. One of the greatest difficulties in a managed system is to get agreement on changes in parities, partly because of the conflicting trade interests at stake. Countries with strong currencies tend to be reluctant to see weaker currencies devalued and their exports undercut. Making changes in small steps should minimize this problem.

If, for example, rates were to be kept in bands of ±2.5 per cent around their stated parities, the convention might be to review them monthly and make changes in 1 per cent steps. (There is an analogy with the way changes in central banks' interest rates are now made.) If any monthly changes in parity were smaller than 2.5 per cent (so that the new parity lay within the old band), the gains from speculation would be greatly reduced.

One way of facilitating the process of adjustment would be to have a 'crawling peg' system, under which parities and bands were automatically adjusted at the end of each period in accordance with a formula based on the actual behaviour of rates in the previous month. For example, if the rate had been consistently below parity, the band would come down, and vice versa. A wholly automatic approach of this kind is, however, in danger of perpetuating the same type of oscillations in rates that we suffer from at the moment. Any movement upwards or downwards would be liable to develop a momentum of its own. It would be better to have a discretionary system, which would pay regard to immediate past trends but not follow them slavishly.

The third key lesson from the ERM experience is the need for adequate intervention arrangements to keep rates within their stated bands. *Ad hoc* intervention by the central banks concerned did not prove adequate. It took time to arrange and the conflict of interest between the Bundesbank and others was often too great. A bilateral arrangement between the Bank of England and the European Central Bank could be more effective, provided it was made binding from the start. But, particularly if more than two currencies were involved, the most effective solution would be to set up *automatic* arrangements with a special intervention fund with adequate borrowing rights. Once the intervention machinery was seen to be effective, it would hardly ever be needed.

Implications for monetary policy

Whilst intervention, rather than interest rate policy, would be the instrument for keeping exchange rates within their stated bands, such a system would mean that the UK (and other participants) would have to keep their interest rates broadly in line with those set by the ECB. While we would not have surrendered our ability to operate a national monetary policy for all time, as we would do by entering EMU, we would, however, have greatly reduced our room to manoeuvre. This is, of course, implicit in any such attempt to ensure greater exchange rate stability. The corollary is that we would have to revert to making greater use of budgetary policy to regulate demand. I see no great objections to that. The fact that the Bank of England's brief reign as independent has coincided with a beneficial upswing in demand without renewed inflation is probably more a matter of world circumstances than the miraculous effects of fine-tuning by 0.25 per cent changes in interest rates! The present fashion of relying solely on interest rates to regulate demand cannot survive in EMU without bringing the structure to near breaking point.

Any moves to stabilize the relation between the pound and the euro must be seen in the wider context of the need for greater exchange rate stability on a global scale. As argued in more detail in chapter 5, there can be no question of any general return to 'fixed' exchange rates on the Bretton Woods pattern; and currency unions are only practicable between countries with a high degree of economic and political convergence. But as with the pound and the euro, we should not fall into the trap of assuming that the only alternatives are the two extremes of a return to fixed rates or a continuation of the present floating rate regime. In this case there is a 'Third Way': that is, a *managed* exchange rate approach. The practicalities of managing rates dictate, however, that any such regime can only be introduced on a two-tier basis, with a combination of regional and global management.

Should the UK join EMU?

A new ERM agreement to stabilize the rate between the pound and the euro would not only benefit industry, but would also have considerable political attractions. An arrangement on these lines should commend itself both to those who believe that we should enter EMU, either in the short or longer term, and those who think we should stay out. For the former it would be a way of establishing the degree of stability against the euro that we formally need before qualifying for entry. For the latter, it would provide an effective alternative to membership. Given the extent to which the political world is divided on the issue, such a course would seem to have considerable political appeal. It is strange that the Government should have gone on record as being categorically opposed to any such move. The Financial Secretary told the Treasury Committee that 'we have absolutely no intention of being in an ERM2 or shadowing the euro or any other such arrangement.'[6] The fact that our previous membership of the old ERM ended in political disaster because we entered at too high an exchange rate should not rule out joining a new managed rate system at a competitive rate. (Perhaps it would help politically if any new arrangement had a different title, e.g. New Exchange Rate System – and was seen as the brain-child of the UK government!) An effective new exchange rate management system would provide an interim means of dealing with the problems of the accession members who are formally committed to eventual membership of EMU. But any such arrangement must be subject to the overriding proviso that the UK (or any other country concerned) enters at a realistic exchange rate.

For my own part, I would see membership of a new ERM as preferable to joining EMU as at present constituted. Joining EMU would mean that our economic policy would be dominated by an independent central bank lacking any form of democratic control and where the use of fiscal policy (certainly in an expansionary direction) has effectively been ruled out. When, as seems both desirable and inevitable, the EMU members eventually establish some form of federal government with responsibility for European economic policy, then the basic political concept surrounding EMU would be more acceptable; but the decision at some point in the future as to whether the UK should join such a federation will be extremely fraught and may well torment us for many decades to come.

Notes

1. *Report on Economic and Monetary Union in the Economic Community* (European Community, 1989).
2. Council Resolution 97/C 236/01.
3. *The Role of Public Finance in European Integration* (European Union, 1977).
4. Austria, Belgium, Germany, Greece, Spain, France, Italy, Luxembourg, Portugal and Sweden have state earnings-related schemes. Denmark, Ireland, the Netherlands and Finland have flat rate schemes.
5. Majocchi, A. and Rey, M., *A Special Financial Support Scheme in EMU: Need and Nature*; Goodhart, C.A.E. and Smith, S., *Stabilisation* (Commission of the European Communities, 1994).
6. Evidence to the House of Commons Treasury Committee hearing on Economic and Monetary Union, 11 July 2000.

Chapter 5

REFORMING THE GLOBAL FINANCIAL SYSTEM

If people like me can crash a currency system, there is certainly something wrong with the system.

George Soros

1. THE THREAT OF INSTABILITY

The ultimate weakness of the New Orthodoxy is that it provides no answer to the instability of the global financial system, which poses a serious threat to industry and jobs throughout the world. Since the Western industrialized countries came through the 1997 Asian crisis relatively unscathed (and indeed benefited from the fall in primary product prices) there has been a tendency in the West to underplay the severity of the crisis and the need for reform. Although they are recovering now, the impact on the countries involved was devastating. Unemployment in Indonesia, Korea and Thailand rose from five million at the end of 1996 to 18 million at the end of 1998; and in Indonesia 17 million more people fell below the $1 a day poverty line. This represents human tragedy on a vast scale. But it was only one in a series of crises. It was preceded by the Mexican crisis in 1995 and followed by the Brazilian and Russian crises in 1998.

It should not be assumed that only developing countries are vulnerable to such events. We are all at risk. The volatility of international capital flows, bubbles in stock market and property prices, and unstable exchange rates can cause problems anywhere. There is always a risk that a slow-down in the American economy could lead to a collapse in stock market prices on Wall Street. A consequent rush of foreign investors to get out of the dollar could hit the American economy and induce a widespread recession. But this is only one of a variety of possible scenarios including for example, the possibility that Japan might not be able to get out of the current recession.

But crises apart, the instability of exchange rates presents serious problems for industry world-wide. The recent problems of the British steel and car industries are only one dramatic example. Multinational firms cannot plan their investment and operations rationally when future exchange rates are so uncertain. The uncertainty inhibits industrial expansion. Manufacturers whose exports become unprofitable close plants and cut their labour force when the exchange rate is high, but do not necessarily expand again directly it falls, because they have no means of knowing whether export sales will remain competitive.

There is an urgent need for fundamental reform of the global financial system. In the immediate aftermath of the Asian crisis, this was widely recognized and there was much talk of the need for a 'new global financial architecture'. But as the threat of a wider recession receded, Western leaders became less concerned about root and branch reform; and finance ministers, for example, soon limited their discussions to what one American commentator called 'interior decoration' rather than 'new architecture'. Official discussion has focused almost exclusively on the need to improve the prudential regulation of banks and other financial institutions, and paid little attention to other aspects of reforming the operation of global financial markets.

Bretton Woods

International economic crises are not a new phenomenon. Major financial crises in the inter-war period contributed to the emergence of mass unemployment in the 1930s, which was a major contributor to the rise in fascism – a good reason for not being complacent about the high levels of unemployment prevalent in many parts of Europe today. In a policy statement as early as 1933, the Labour Party said that 'the world has become a single economic unit and governments must pursue an active policy of International Economic Co-operation'.[1] As this attitude took hold, and with the achievement of full employment during World War II, there grew a widespread resolve among the Allies to establish a more stable international economic system, which would help to prevent a recurrence

94

of mass unemployment. The result was the Bretton Woods Agreement of 1944. The spirit of the time was exemplified by Keynes's concluding speech to the Conference, of which he had been the prime architect:

> If we can continue in a larger task as we have begun in this limited task, there is hope for the world... We have been learning to work together. If we can so continue, this nightmare, in which most of us present have spent too much of our lives, will be over. The brotherhood of man will become more than a phrase.[2]

But over the last 50 years, international economic cooperation has weakened rather than strengthened, despite the fact that 'globalization' has made it more imperative than ever. The development of more effective international institutions, not only for economic policy, but also in such fields as the environment and peacekeeping, presents the major political challenge of our time. We can only tackle these problems if national governments are prepared to work more closely together.

Although the world economic system has changed considerably since then, we are still living in the shadow of the Bretton Woods Agreement. The two leading international economic institutions, the International Monetary Fund and the World Bank, were set up under that Agreement and the constitution under which they operate has remained to a large extent unchanged – although their actual method of operation has evolved in a manner that their founders did not envisage.

A prime objective at Bretton Woods was to devise an international payments system which would help countries to maintain full employment. To this end it set up a 'stable' exchange rate system and arrangements to enable countries in balance of payments difficulties to borrow from the new International Monetary Fund. The so-called 'fixed' exchange rate system was intended to provide a basis for stability, whilst allowing countries to adjust their rates from time to time when they got out of line. In principle this meant that countries with chronic surpluses should adjust their exchange rates upwards (to curb their exports and encourage imports) as well as those in deficit adjusting their rates downwards. But in practice the onus of adjustment nearly always fell on those in deficit, who found they had to devalue under pressure of circumstances and in conditions of crisis. The symmetry in adjustment between creditors and debtors sought by Keynes and others never materialized.

At the time of Bretton Woods, strict exchange controls over all payments, whether current or capital, were part of wartime arrangements. The Agreement provided that controls on imports and other current transactions should be liberalized as soon as possible, but controls on capital movements could remain in place. (The case for free trade in goods and services among industrialized countries was generally accepted, assisted by US pressure to liberalize dollar imports; but Keynes, in particular, had seen volatile capital movements as a major source of financial instability in the inter-war period, and their control as a continuing necessity.) With the restoration of peace-time conditions, controls on current transactions were gradually relaxed. The fixed exchange rate regime lasted until the early 1970s when it began to break up – partly because of the difficulty of agreeing on changes in rates when the existing structure was no longer appropriate, and partly because of the increasing importance of capital movements in putting pressure on, or determining, exchange rates. We then entered a period in which exchange rates were for the most part 'floating' (i.e. determined mainly or entirely by activity in currency markets); although some, particularly developing, countries 'pegged' their rates to a leading or neighbouring country's currency, such as the dollar. It is in this unstable world that we still find ourselves today.

The advantage to countries like the UK of abandoning the fixed-rate system was that they no longer faced devaluation crises such as we experienced in 1949 and 1967, and again in a different context when we left the ERM in 1992. But a major disadvantage of the new regime is that exchange rates have become markedly unstable, and bear no necessary relation to relative costs in different countries, as the recent punishingly high level of sterling testifies. Exchange rates nowadays are determined by the enormous volume of short-term financial transactions, which completely dwarfs the volume of transactions carried out for international trade.

Volatile movements of short-term capital into and out of countries not only affect exchange rates, but also prices of assets such as shares and property. Typically, investment in a particular country or countries, such as those in the so-called 'Asian miracle', becomes highly fashionable; money pours in; stock market and property prices soar; and the exchange rate comes under upward pressure. Some catalytic event then leads to a reversal of sentiment; money moves out; asset prices collapse; and the exchange rate plunges.

The Asian Crisis

The Asian crisis of 1997 was a dramatic illustration of these dangers. Before it struck, the spectacular speed of industrialization and economic growth in Korea and other East Asian countries became familiarly known as the 'East Asian Miracle' – the title of a World Bank report on their achievements. Their rates of growth of production were much higher than most other countries; inflation was in single figures and their budgets were either in surplus or had small sustainable deficits. The general perception of these economies as highly successful led to a heavy inflow of foreign investment which enabled them to run substantial current deficits in their balance of payments. But these deficits left them vulnerable to a reversal of such capital movements. When it occurred, there was a dramatic turnaround in Western opinion, with constant references to 'crony capitalism' and 'structural weaknesses'. The crisis provided an excuse to try to force those countries to abandon any degree of public planning and control and adopt the neo-liberal model of capitalism or so-called 'Washington consensus', driven by the 'US Treasury-Wall Street complex' with its emphasis on privatization and liberalization of financial markets. Attention was initially focused primarily on the supposed structural weaknesses in these countries' economies, rather than those of the world financial system in which they operated. As time passed, however, it was increasingly acknowledged that the economic devastation inflicted on these countries reflected structural faults in the way international markets and financial institutions operate, rather than their particular form of capitalism.

Countries at all stages of development and with a variety of forms of industrial and financial organization are now vulnerable to the vagaries of the financial markets. Far from the distinguishing features of the Asian economies being a cause of the crises, the premature pressure on them to follow the Western pattern and liberalize capital flows into and out of their countries was a major contributing factor.[3]

97

The fragility of the exchange rate regime was evident in the way their currencies went down like dominoes in a matter of days. The process started on 15 May 1997 when Thailand introduced capital and exchange controls in an effort to maintain its exchange rate peg to the dollar, after a succession of speculative attacks on the baht in 1996 and early 1997. Thailand was suffering from a large current account deficit, high short-term foreign debt, the collapse of a property price bubble and a loss of competitiveness resulting in part from the rise in the dollar against the yen. Equity prices had been falling. On 2 July 1997 Thailand abandoned its exchange rate peg and allowed the baht to float, which raised doubts about exchange rates elsewhere in the region. The Philippines had also been maintaining a *de facto* peg to the dollar, and after seeking briefly to defend it, the authorities floated the peso on 11 July 1997. Malaysia came under pressure and the ringgit was allowed to depreciate. In Indonesia the rupiah fell sharply within the intervention band on 21 July and was floated on 14 August. The Singapore dollar and the new Taiwan dollar weakened moderately in July and the Hong Kong dollar came under temporary attack in early August. By mid-October, the baht and rupiah had depreciated by over 30 per cent against the dollar, and the ringgit and peso by over 20 per cent. The Korean won also came under pressure. Contagion was rapid.

As the crisis developed, equity prices throughout the region fell sharply. By December the fall for Asian developing countries as a whole was over 40 per cent. The combined effect of falling stock market prices and currency depreciation led to spectacular losses for foreign investors with falls from highs to lows in dollar terms of 89 per cent in Indonesia, 82 per cent in Malaysia and 85 per cent in Thailand.[4] Financial developments in the stock markets and currency markets were linked to a series of solvency crises in financial institutions and industrial companies across the region. In May 1997, Thailand's largest finance company, Finance One, closed along with 15 other cash-strapped finance firms. By December, 56 of the 58 finance companies were permanently shut. In Indonesia 16 banks in difficulties closed at the beginning of November. In just a few months the financial systems of these countries had been brought to their knees.

Bankruptcies seem to have been a particularly important factor in Korea. Whereas the economies of the developing countries in South East Asia could be said to be intrinsically vulnerable to attack, the Korean economy was much more advanced, and in industrial terms a major player on the world stage. But the Korean chaebols (or conglomerates) had financed their expansion by excessive reliance on short-term foreign loans which left them vulnerable. In January 1997, Hannbo Steel collapsed under $6 billion in foreign debt – the first bankruptcy of a leading conglomerate in a decade. In March another steel company, Sammi, failed. In July, Korea's third largest car maker, Kia, asked for emergency loans and was eventually nationalized after the banks refused additional credit.

The reversal of the flow of bank credit played a major role in the Asian crisis, accounting for the greater part of the changes in the flow of private capital. Between 1996 and 1998 there was a reversal of total net private capital flows of $108 billion to the five crisis countries, Korea, Indonesia, Malaysia, Philippines and Thailand (from an inflow of $62 billion to an outflow of $45 billion in 1998). The corresponding change in foreign bank loans was $114 billion (from an inflow of $46 billion to an outflow of $65 billion).

In the autumn of 1997, the 'Asian flu' spread to Brazil. Foreign investors lost confidence; there was a sharp fall in stock market prices and downward pressure on the real. In the summer of 1998 Russia came into the firing line. Stock markets were in a state of turmoil and the ruble came under heavy pressure. The Russian economy is in such a poor state anyhow, that its involvement in such a crisis may seem of little significance. But the moral is that volatile capital movements present a threat to a wide variety of economies.

Tackling the problem

Successive international economic crises have all had their own special features, and we should not make the mistake of basing proposals for future reform solely on the experience of any one episode. Nevertheless the closely inter-related phenomena of volatile capital flows, asset price bubbles and unstable exchange rates tend to be common factors. We need to tackle the problem of reforming and strengthening the global financial system on a broad front, so that measures to damp down the volatility of capital movements, asset prices and exchange rates all reinforce each other.

Financial market activity is not (or should not be) an end in itself, but a means of providing a service to industry and investors. Its prime functions are to provide efficient means of financing trade in goods and services and linking potential investors to industries needing capital. If exchange rates, bank lending and stock market prices are excessively volatile, financial markets are not performing those functions efficiently and need to be reviewed.

2. IMPROVING FINANCIAL REGULATION

A key element in the evolution of international financial crises is the so-called 'herd behaviour' of financial institutions and investors, in particular their tendency to follow each other into investing in whatever country or market is fashionable at the moment. This can lead (as in the Asian crisis) into excessive bank lending and over-borrowing in a particular country, or group of countries, with each lender paying insufficient heed to the extent of their collective total commitment. This gives rise to a two-fold risk to the lender. The initial risk is that the borrowing bank or firm may have difficulty in meeting the interest payments or repaying the loan. The secondary or 'systemic' risk is that the group of borrowers as a whole may get into difficulty, thus making it more difficult for each of them to meet their obligations. This in turn puts additional pressure on the lenders to recover their money. Recent crises have highlighted this problem and focused attention on the role of the regulators of financial institutions in reducing such risks by improved 'prudential' regulation.

In 1999 finance ministers in the G7 group of leading industrial countries set up a new Financial Stability Forum to co-ordinate the work of (mainly national) regulatory organizations, under the chairmanship of the General Manager of the Bank for International Settlements in Basel. The supervisory code for banks will continue to be the responsibility of the Basel Committee on Banking Supervision, which in January 2001 issued a consultative document proposing a New Capital Accord with revised provisions for the 'capital backing' (or amount of capital) banks should have available to absorb potential losses on different types of loans. These provisions play an important part in determining the pattern of bank loans, because in the interests of profitability banks wish to maximize their loans in relation to their capital base, subject of course to what they regard as the risks involved. An important illustration of the effect of the existing Basel provisions was the high proportion of bank lending to Asia that was for periods of one year or less. By mid-summer 1996 bank loans maturing within one year made up 70 per cent of the total for South Korea, 69 per cent for Thailand, 62 per cent for Indonesia, but 47 per cent for Malaysia. This reflected the fact that under the previous Basel rules, loans for less than a year required only one-fifth of the capital backing that longer-term loans required. The rationale of this was that individual banks were seen to be at less risk with loans that the borrowers knew they would have to repay or renew in the short-term. The weakness was that while this might be true for any one bank on its own, it was not the case when they all refused to renew one-year loans at much the same time.

There is clearly a case for keeping the pattern of capital backing requirements under review in order to reflect up-to-date assessments of the risks involved in lending to different countries or in particular forms. But it seems unlikely that the regulators, who are in close touch with those they regulate, will be altogether immune to the vagaries of investment fashion. More fundamental than the pattern of capital banking requirements is the general level. A basic weakness of the international financial system today is excessive 'leverage': that is the ability to achieve a large gain (or loss) from a small stake. Take the domestic example of someone who buys a house putting down 10 per cent in cash and raising a 90 per cent mortgage, i.e. a leverage of 10:1. If house prices rise by 10 per cent they will have doubled their original deposit when they sell. But if prices go down by 10 per cent, they will have nothing left. The financial press recently carried a series of advertisements directed at private investors: 'Trade Shares at Margin . . . Deposit as low as 20%.' Similar leverage exists throughout the financial system, both directly through the use of credit to buy financial assets and through the development of 'derivatives', which make it possible to make a large bet on asset prices, interest rates or exchange rates with a small stake. Products developed to enable people to 'hedge' (i.e. safeguard themselves against changes in interest rates, exchange rates, asset prices or creditworthiness) became new fields for speculation by others.

A prime example of the consequences of excessive leverage was the collapse of the Long Term Capital Management hedge fund in 1998, which had to be rescued by a consortium of leading financial institutions – despite the fact that it depended on the work of two Nobel prize-winning economists who, *The Economist* prematurely rhapsodized, had 'turned risk management from a guessing game into a science'! It was operating on a leverage ratio of over 25:1 with assets nominally valued at about $120 billion and a capital base of only $4.8 billion.[5] If other financial institutions had not come to its aid, the sale of its assets would have led to a sharp fall in prices, which would in turn have placed others in difficulties.

A major objective of any reform of financial markets should be to reduce the amount of leverage in the system. One way of doing so would be to raise permanently the general level of capital backing required under the Basel agreement (as well as keeping the pattern under review) – something the proposed New Capital Accord notably fails to do. But there is also a need for a wider international review of the use of derivatives and the role of credit in world stock markets. Such a review needs to be undertaken before there is a major stock market crisis, rather than as with the 1929 Wall Street crash, when the Federal Reserve tightened up on bank lending for stock purchases after the event. Banks are unlikely to welcome any curb on their ability to lend, regarding it as a threat to their profitability. But in the long run such restrictions may well save them from themselves.

The argument for taking precautions against such economic dangers is not (as is so often suggested) invalidated because the threatened danger has not materialized in the period since such precautions were proposed. If that were a valid approach in other walks of life, few safety precautions would ever be taken. If we tell our children to 'mind how they cross the road', the admonition is not needless merely because they scamper across a few times without getting run over! Whatever the precise probability of a stock market crash with disastrous effects on industry and jobs, it is only sensible to take precautions now to reduce the chances of it happening.

3. THE FLOW OF CAPITAL TO DEVELOPING COUNTRIES

Capital controls

Recent crises belie the neo-liberal thesis that removing restrictions on the international flow of capital would benefit all concerned. Many developing countries have paid a devastating price in terms of instability for any temporary increase in the inflow of foreign capital. Pressure on developing or newly industrialized countries from the Washington institutions and Western finance ministers to liberalize their capital markets has exacted a heavy toll in bankruptcies and lost jobs. It is time to rethink the official attitude to capital controls in order to reduce the instability of short-term capital movements, and re-examine ways of improving and stabilizing the flow of long-term investment.

It may be significant in this context that the IMF have now published a staff report, *Country Experiences with the Use and Liberalization of Capital Controls*, which expresses an unexpectedly open attitude to the use of such controls. Their review of the various types of control adopted in different countries in varying circumstances suggests that no one pattern of control is universally most effective. The most acceptable have been those which in effect use the price mechanism rather than quantitative controls or outright prohibition of particular activities. Chile, Colombia and Malaysia have been the prime examples.

In 1991 the Chilean government imposed an Unrenumerated Reserve Requirement of 20 per cent on foreign loans. This had to be deposited at the central bank, interest free, and left there until maturity for credits of less than a year, and for 12 months for credits over a year. In the following year the requirement was raised to 30 per cent for a year irrespective of loan maturity. In 1998 this was reduced to 10 per cent and then abolished; but foreign investors had to keep their money in the country for over a year. Similar measures were introduced in Colombia. The Chilean measures effectively imposed a tax (in the guise of a loss of interest) which was steepest on short-term capital inflows and tapered downwards as the period of the loan lengthened.

Malaysia has recently employed a more direct approach. In 1998, as

103

part of a wide range of exchange and capital controls, the authorities imposed a 12-month waiting period on the repatriation of ringitt proceeds from sales of securities held in external accounts. In February 1999 they replaced this with a graduated levy on the proceeds of repatriating port-folio investment, ranging from 30 per cent for assets held less than seven months to zero for assets held for over a year.

Such controls avoid detailed regulation and can help curb short-term speculative movements, although the longer they are in force, the more adept investors become at finding ways to evade them. IMF policy on capital controls needs to be revised in two respects. The first is that developing countries should no longer be pressed to open their capital markets to international investors more rapidly than their governments consider prudent. The second is that their use of capital controls in vari-ous forms when inflows seem excessive, or crises threaten, should be regarded as acceptable behaviour.

Long-term capital

Apart from damping down unstable movements of short-term capital, the principal need of developing countries is a stable flow of long-term capital. In practice this depends mainly on foreign direct investment (FDI) in firms or plants in those countries. The encouragement of FDI does, however, carry with it problems when the control of firms in one country comes under the control of headquarters situated elsewhere. This is, of course, not just a problem for developing countries, as Britain's own motor industry shows. The spread of overseas control is in danger of further weakening firms' concern for the people and institutions in areas in which they operate – a trend strongly associated with the short-term approach of financial interests to the firms in which they are involved.

Whereas direct investment is a relatively stable source of foreign capital, portfolio investment in equity or debt issued by companies in developing countries is essentially footloose. Whilst such investment may be long-term as far as the companies themselves are concerned, it may be very volatile from the point of view of the country as a whole if foreigners start to sell their holdings – although a wave of selling will only result in an actual outflow of capital if foreigners can sell their investments to domestic investors; in so far as they unload them on other foreign investors, such sales will only result in falling prices. Either way the country concerned will suffer some currency outflow and pressure on the exchange rate, and falling stock market prices will depress domestic spending and make it more difficult for those firms to raise further capital.

It is time for a fresh examination of the role of the World Bank and its affiliate, the International Finance Corporation (IFC), in promoting the flow of development capital, particularly to poorer countries. In this connection George Soros' proposals for insuring loans to developing countries could provide a basis for evolving new ways of stimulating a steady flow of capital at a time when confidence is low. Soros proposed that a new institution:

> would explicitly guarantee international loans and credits up to defined limits. The borrowing countries would be obliged to provide data on all borrowings, public or private, insured or not. This would enable the authority to set a ceiling on the amounts it was willing to insure. Up to those amounts, the countries concerned would be able to access international capital markets at prime rates plus a modest fee. Beyond these limits, the creditors would be at risk.[6]

Lenders would be obliged to pay an insurance premium to cover the risk, and the cost of this would be passed on to the borrower.

Soros acknowledges the problem of rationing the availability of insured credit within the recipient country and suggests that this should be done by competition among authorized banks (who would presumably profit from the difference between insured and uninsured lending rates). There are obviously considerable problems in devising a workable scheme, not least determining a reasonable level of premiums. What sort of borrowers would be eligible for guaranteed loans? Would the availability of guarantees depend on the apparent creditworthiness of the borrower? Despite these unanswered questions, the insurance concept deserves further consideration, including the possible role of regional development banks.

Private investment in developing countries needs to be buttressed by official development finance in the form of grants and loans for investment in basic social capital such as public utilities, and as finance for the provision of guarantees and investment insurance for industrial investment. This is particularly important for poorer countries. Official grants and loans have become relatively less important in recent years. Since the mid-1980s the flow of such finance to developing countries had declined from over half total net capital inflows in the period 1983–9 to only 20 per cent in 1990–98, approximately half in grants and half in loans. The shift in emphasis from official to private capital has been to the detriment of poorer countries. But with the decline in private investment following the Asian crises, official development finance assumes increasing importance and new ways need to be found to fund it. The Tobin Tax (discussed in the next section) is one possible source of additional finance for such purposes.

4. THE ROLE OF TAXATION

One measure which would help to damp down excessive speculative activity in currency markets and raise money for international purposes is the Tobin Tax – a small tax, say 0.1 per cent, on foreign exchange transactions. This was first proposed by the American professor James Tobin in 1972 as a means of curbing currency speculation, but in recent years increasing attention has been paid to its revenue-raising potential for international purposes, such as increasing aid to developing countries or environmental measures, and it has now gained the support of George Soros. The growth of foreign exchange trading has meant that its revenue potential is increasing rapidly. Revenue estimates depend on how effective the tax would be in reducing market activity; but on the basis of 1995 turnover, the potential revenue has been put at between $150 and 200 billion a year[7] depending on how far the new tax reduced market activity. Between 1995 and 1998, however, the average daily turnover of foreign exchange transactions including derivatives rose by a third. (Trading in traditional foreign exchange instruments rose by one-quarter; trade in derivatives nearly doubled.)[8] Thus the potential revenue today would be over $200 billion.

Imposing such a tax would raise problems of coverage, in particular the treatment of various derivatives. But compared with many existing taxes, it would be relatively simple. Only a fairly small number of institutions are

106

involved and the tax calculations could be built into their computerized systems. The real problem is to secure the necessary international agreement to introduce it, the rules under which it would operate and the rate at which it would be charged.

One suggestion is that as an incentive to take part, countries which levied the tax might keep some of the proceeds for their own use; possibly in varying proportion according to their stage of development. As one-third of all transactions take place in the London market, this could be of particular interest to the UK. (Wider considerations apart, any British Chancellor is liable to be torn between the revenue-raising possibilities involved and the strength of the financial lobby against any such tax!) If the tax were levied according to the market in which the transaction took place, all countries would have an incentive to participate, rather than become off-shore tax havens. In so far as tax havens did remain, a penalty tax could be levied on all transactions with them by markets in the participating countries.

The role of the tax in reducing speculative activity would be one of damping down the vast volume of day-to-day speculative activity, but it would not be an effective antidote to speculation on major changes in exchange rates. A very high proportion of transactions are for periods of less than seven days and are intended to exploit minor changes in exchange rates or interest rates. An indication of the order of magnitude involved is that a tax of 0.1 per cent (equivalent to 0.2 per cent on the sale and then purchase of a currency) would mean that transactions to exploit very short-term differences of interest rates of less than 10 per cent a year (0.2 per cent a week) would no longer be profitable. On the other hand, a tax at this rate would be immaterial in speculating against a currency liable to devalue by 10 per cent in a matter of days or weeks.

The extent to which it is desirable to damp down short-term activity in currency markets depends on a judgement as to how far such activity is doing industry a service by providing a more stable market (as orthodox opinion has hitherto asserted), or how far such market activity has itself become a cause of instability. A standard reference book on currency trading gives the game away when it cautions aspiring dealers that 'there are few worse scenarios for currency traders than a relatively flat market... The solution to the problem is options trading.'[9]. At the present time it is clear that such activity has become excessive and destabilizing. Short-term transactions are a major factor in the herd-like movements into and out of currencies. When currencies are rising (or falling), the odds on the movement continuing in the same direction for a few more hours or days are always very strong, and as dealers chase the currency up (or down), such short-term speculation becomes self-validating.

Taxing financial transactions

The proposal to tax foreign exchange transactions goes back nearly 30 years. Since then the growth of global financial markets has exposed our economies to a growing threat of instability not merely from exchange rate fluctuations and crises, but also in stock markets. The use of taxation to damp down speculative activity needs to be considered in relation to a much wider range of financial transactions. It has long been considered acceptable to tax purchases on goods and services (e.g. by VAT); but it has been argued that financial transactions should broadly speaking be left untaxed to make markets more 'liquid'. It is clear now, however, that on the contrary, financial markets have become too liquid, and any taxation that reduced the volume of transactions would be desirable, rather then the reverse. It is interesting that the Stock Exchange in campaigning for the abolition of 0.5 per cent stamp duty on share deals argued that this would raise trading volume by 40 per cent.[10] In so far as this is not merely a transfer of trading from one market to another, this seems an overwhelming reason against doing so. The moral rather is that the Chancellor should seek international agreement to harmonize taxes on such transactions – an initiative for which his fellow finance ministers might well be grateful.

It is, becoming, increasingly apparent that taxes on financial transactions need to be harmonized on a global (not just a regional) basis, now that such activity can take place anywhere in the world – whereas while sales taxes on goods need some degree of harmonization in areas between which they can be easily transferred (e.g. bringing wine or beer across the Channel), this does not have to be global. Taxes on financial activity and the mobile rich will, however, increasingly require internationally agreed rules and rates. This is an area of international co-operation which has barely taken off, but which will become increasingly important in the coming decade.

New international machinery will be needed to handle both tax harmonization in these fields and any new international taxes, such as the Tobin Tax. While the Tobin Tax was originally mooted as a way of curbing speculative activity, it has recently been put forward by War on Want and other NGOs as a means of financing international aid and development, and would be an appropriate means of raising additional finance for the UN and other international agencies.

5. MANAGING EXCHANGE RATES

Exchange rates lie at the heart of the global financial regime. They set the terms on which countries trade each other's goods and services, and the level of rates can have a powerful effect on industrial output and employment. From industry's point of view the two objectives are that rates should be competitive and stable. Under the present regime of floating rates, neither objective is assured – as British industry is uncomfortably aware. Foreign exchange markets do not (as economic theorists once suggested) adjust rates so that countries' international payments come into balance – they never did. But today the overwhelming determinant is the movement of short-term capital. The result is that when it is fashionable, a currency like sterling may become overvalued and its exports uncompetitive, with disastrous consequences for many of its industries. But when sterling comes down, firms will not automatically increase export capacity again and take on more staff, because they will have no means of telling where the exchange rate will be in six months' or a year's time. Such a situation is starkly at odds with the development of multinational industrial companies who find themselves unable to plan future investment or operations rationally when variations in exchange rates can alter the relative costs of plants in different countries from month to month in an unpredictable fashion. An unjustifiably high exchange rate in one country may lead to production cuts or plant closures in that country with disastrous economic and social consequences for the people and areas concerned.

The answer to the problem of achieving a more stable system is not to go back to a fixed-rate regime. Both fixed-rate and free-floating systems suffer from serious weaknesses. The major weakness of the 'fixed'-rate system is the difficulty of adjusting rates when relative costs in different countries get out of line. Such adjustments are generally delayed until they are long overdue and then forced on the country by a run on its currency and consequent devaluation in crisis conditions. Industry suffers from the delay in adjustment and finance ministers are compelled to commit virtual political suicide. To deter speculation they are forced to deny that devaluation is a possibility until a run on the currency market makes it inevitable. Their credibility is then in tatters. No wonder they tend to prefer floating rates: even if industry suffers, finance ministers do not get the blame!

One answer to the quest for stability is to form a currency union, such as the EMU, which effectively fixes the rates of the participants for all time by adopting a common currency. But this is only a practical route for countries which have achieved a high degree of integration, and even then may cause serious strains if costs in one area get out of line. A more general solution is to adopt some form of 'managed' rate system, under which countries seek to achieve target rates for their currencies: these can be either informal and unstated, or publicly stated parities and bands, as in the ERM.

As suggested in chapter 4, the history of the ERM highlights the two fundamental difficulties that have to be overcome if a system on similar lines is to operate successfully elsewhere. The first is the difficulty of getting agreement on adjustments in rates. The second is the need for an effective mechanism for intervening in the markets to keep rates within their stated bands. The break-up of the ERM in September 1992 reflected the inability of the members to agree on such changes and their inability to resist speculative pressure when their increasingly unrealistic rates came under attack. These two problems are interlinked, because an essential prerequisite for being able to resist speculation is that the rates should be seen to be realistic and sustainable.

One way to overcome these problems is to review the rates at relatively frequent intervals, say monthly, and make only relatively small adjustments in rates. (There is an analogy with the way central banks review interest rates once a month.) For example, if the agreement was that rates would be kept within a band of ± 2.5 per cent of their stated parities and parities were moved up or down by 1 per cent after the monthly meetings, the new parity would still lie within the old band and the spot rate the next day might be no lower than it was before. This would considerably limit the scope for making major speculative gains. The broad aim would be to keep 'real' rates (i.e. rates after allowing for differing rates of inflation) broadly stable.

The second innovation would be that intervention in currency markets to stabilize rates should be *automatic* rather than discretionary. Discretionary intervention involves *ad hoc* consultation and action by central banks. It takes time and their foreign exchange resources are limited in relation to market turnover. Automatic intervention would be most effective if it were the responsibility of a special stabilization fund set up with adequate resources for this task, rather than left to co-operation between central banks. Making the same committee of central bank and government officials responsible both for setting rates and running the stabilization fund should ensure that the rates are realistic and maintainable. Once the system is seen to be effective, the stabilization fund should in practice have little cause to intervene.

A two-tier approach

A system of this type, and indeed any managed rate system, formal or informal, can only operate effectively among a number of participants small enough to be able to reach mutual agreement on rates. It would not be practical on a world-wide scale. This suggests that the achievement of greater exchange rate stability depends on a two-tier approach, with arrangements to manage rates both within regional country groupings and also between such regions. Such a movement is likely to take the form initially of developing regional arrangements in Europe, America and Asia, based on the euro (and sterling), the dollar and the yen, and then a 'tri-polar' system for managing the rates between these three groupings. As suggested in chapter 4, the EU grouping would operate a new ERM mechanism on these lines to stabilize the relation between the euro and EU members outside EMU, including sterling.

In Asia, under the Chiang Mai initiative, 13 countries have agreed arrangements to monitor foreign exchange markets, with swap and repurchase mechanisms to aid currencies in difficulties. China, with its huge foreign exchange reserves of over $150 billion, has now agreed to participate and arrangements are in hand to formalize the present *ad hoc* arrangements. The US, which shot down an earlier Japanese plan for an Asian monetary fund is supporting the new initiative.

In Latin America, the current issue is 'dollarization', i.e. other countries adopting the US dollar as their own currency. This raises serious political and economic problems for both sides, since American monetary policy would become the monetary policy for the dollarized countries without their participation in the Federal Reserve System. A more flexible form of mutual currency management on the lines outlined above would in the longer run be a more widely acceptable alternative.

Stability at the global and regional levels is inter-related. It would, for example, be much more practical to maintain a stable relationship between the pound and the euro if the euro were more stable relative to the dollar. Similarly in the East, it would be easier for Asian countries to have stable rates vis-à-vis the yen if the yen were stable relative to the dollar. The regional arrangements would probably vary from continent to continent, but there is a strong case for stated parities and bands (reviewed say, monthly) and automatic stabilization arrangements.

If exchange rate parities are to be determined by discussion between the participants in the system, two conditions are essential. The first is that on entering the system countries' rates must be at a reasonable level. It is essential to avoid countries entering at unrealistically high rates which damage their industry and cannot be maintained, as happened when sterling entered the ERM in 1990. The danger of doing so is greatest when financial interests take precedence over those of industry. There is always a clash between financial interests who want to see a currency 'strong' and industry which wants it to be 'competitive'. But as Winston Churchill wrote before he succumbed to Treasury and Bank of England pressure and made the mistake of going back on the gold standard in 1925 at the pre-war exchange rate, 'I would rather see Finance less proud and Industry more content.'[11]

The second and more complex condition is that any national discussion of exchange rates must be based on a view as to the desired pattern of payments between the countries concerned. Where most members of the group are more or less in payments balance, this is not of prime concern, but where there are countries with substantial deficits or surpluses, there has to be a view (tacit or overt) as to whether the continuation of these surpluses and deficits is acceptable in setting rates, or whether rates should be adjusted to reduce the imbalance.

The prime example of this arises in considering the rate between the yen and the dollar at a time when the US is running a large current deficit (over $400 billion in 2000) and Japan a substantial surplus (about $120 billion in 2000). Until recently, US expansion was the 'locomotive' of growth in demand throughout the world while the Japanese economy faltered badly. But early in 2001 the US economy appeared to be weakening and the Japanese economy still showed no signs of recovery. A stronger yen would make it more difficult to get the Japanese economy expanding again. But in the longer run, over, say, a five-year period, the continuation of the US deficit at recent levels seems unsustainable. Its continuation depends on the willingness of investors in other countries to fund it by buying US bonds or shares, and investing in industry or property there. A setback on Wall Street, or a loss in confidence in the dollar, could reduce, or even reverse, this flow, creating a serious financial crisis. In the longer run the US deficit must come down and the Japanese surplus, which is to some extent its mirror image, must also come down. This means that sooner or later the dollar must come down and the yen go up. Agreement on this will be a delicate matter and require careful timing. The relationship of the yen and the dollar with the euro will be less difficult because the European surplus is less significant.

Similarly within regions, there will need to be consideration and agreement on the pattern of payments between participating countries – in other words regional as well as global payment strategies.

Fiscal and monetary policy

One corollary of moving into a more stable system of managed exchange rates would be that countries would no longer be free to use monetary policy as their prime means of managing demand. Interest rates in different countries would have to be kept broadly in line, subject to differences in their rates of inflation. (Their general level would reflect global economic conditions with particular reference to the state of the US economy.) Budgetary policy would then become the main tool available to national governments for regulating demand in accordance with differing national circumstances – as it must *a fortiori* in a currency union like EMU with a single currency and monetary policy. Greater use of fiscal policy would run counter to the prevailing political and economic fashion inherited from the monetarist 1980s, but it is a natural consequence of globalization of international financial markets, if industry is not to pay a heavy price (as at present) in terms of exchange rate instability.

6. THE FUTURE OF INTERNATIONAL ECONOMIC INSTITUTIONS

Crisis management

Whatever improvements are made in prudential regulation and other fields, crises may still occur. Contingency plans are needed to deal with them, including agreement in advance on the machinery for managing such crises. When the Asian crisis came, no such coherent management structure for dealing with it existed.

It is important to distinguish three different strands in international crises of this nature.

1. The lack of liquidity or the threat of insolvency facing banks or other major financial institutions.
2. Sovereign debt default, i.e. the inability of national governments to meet debt repayments or interest when they fall due.
3. Foreign exchange crises putting critical pressure on a country's, or several countries', exchange rate and foreign exchange reserves.

The provision of liquidity to the banking system and the rescue of failing national banks is primarily a function of national central bankers and regulatory authorities. But when the institutions are effectively international, or so large that their collapse would have international ramifications, international (rather than purely national) action is required. When the Long Term Capital Management hedge fund collapsed in 1998, a group of American banks, with the Federal Reserve in the background, formed an *ad hoc* group to deal with the situation. The question today is whether such major international operations should be made the responsibility of the IMF or any new international regulatory authority. The recently created Financial Stability Forum in Basel hardly qualifies for this task, as it is essentially only a policy co-ordinating body.

The question of dealing with debt default has been under discussion for some time without agreement on any general approach. The initial objective must be to ensure if possible that the debtor country can meet its obligations, if necessary with assistance from the IMF. Failing that the aim must be to seek agreement between the debtor and creditors for an orderly 'debt workout', i.e. agreement to stretch out the schedule of capital or interest payments. It is crucial so far as possible to solve the problem in such a way as to avoid a general crisis of confidence in the debt of countries believed to be similarly situated.

Dealing with foreign exchange crises is primarily the task of the IMF. There needs, however, to be a distinction between a country's need to borrow from the IMF because (a) it has a balance of payments deficit and (b) there has been a run on its reserves for speculative reasons. The two have, of course, always been connected. Before capital movements were liberalized, sterling crises, for example, tended to reflect balance of payments deficits, but were then precipitated by sales of sterling. Today speculative pressures can dwarf the effects of payments deficits, and we need to rethink the traditional approach that exchange-rate problems are primarily a matter for the country concerned to solve, with some help from the IMF, and possibly other central banks, as a last resort. Exchange rates are essentially a *mutual* affair between a country and its trading partners – something which is much clearer when considering groups of countries than the world as a whole.

Maintenance of an existing pattern of exchange rates should be re-garded as a matter for both the individual country under pressure and its main trading partners. This will become of increasing significance with any move towards managing exchange rates, informal or formal – hence the proposal above that an essential feature of any formal managed sys-tem is the creation of a new Stability Fund committed to automatic inter-vention in currency markets to maintain the agreed rates. This signifies the need to distinguish between (a) the IMF's traditional role of lending to countries in deficit, and (b) the role of market intervention to maintain exchange-rate stability – a function in which strong countries must in effect help the weak, because the latter are least able to intervene effectively in adverse market conditions.

Most of the proposals now under discussion for reforming the IMF, such as the Meltzer Report[12] to the US Congress, are based on a long outdated view of the problems of global financial instability. They see them essentially in terms of individual countries getting into difficulties and needing assistance from the Fund, rather than as breakdowns of the world financial system as a whole. In updating the remit of the Fund, its role should be seen primarily as that of keeping the international financial system operating smoothly, and its country funding as only a part of that responsibility.

Reforming international institutions

A prime weakness of the present system is the way in which the IMF is able to force inappropriate policy prescriptions on countries in difficulties. This takes two forms. The first is to prescribe deflationary budgetary or monetary measures to countries already threatened with rising unemployment (as they did in Indonesia and Thailand) under the pretext of 'restoring confidence'. This runs counter to the original purpose of the IMF which was to provide support for countries in difficulties to enable them to avoid the orthodox prescription of deflation which had such disastrous consequences in the inter-war period.

The second feature is pressing for so-called 'structural reforms', such as privatization. It is totally undemocratic for the US and other Western countries who dominate the IMF to force their own neo-liberal economic ideology on other countries who wish to choose a different path. The Fund and Bank should recognize the case for diversity of institutional and economic frameworks in different countries, not insist that everyone should adopt one uniform model.

In addition to changes in policy at the IMF and World Bank, there is a need to reconsider their roles more generally, and their relation to other international organizations in the economic field, in particular United Nations organizations and the OEECD, many of which seem to have outlived their usefulness. The problem is to reach a workable compromise between the realities of power and the democracy of numbers: in effect the balance between the US and other leading industrialized countries on the one hand, and the rest of the world on the other. At the present time, the developing countries and their massive populations are under-represented in the decision-making structure. This tends to be accentuated by the fact that effective decision-making frequently requires finance ministers to meet in small groups, such as G7, which are almost always composed predominantly or entirely of representatives from the leading industrial countries.

One development which could improve the balance is the emergence of more effective regional organizations. Europe has gone furthest down this road with the evolution of the EU and now the EMU. It illustrates the way that economic integration, active regional economic governance and political cohesion go hand in hand. The economic and political power of any regional organization depends to a large extent on the scope of the duties it has to undertake. The proposal in an earlier chapter that countries should establish regional arrangements for managing exchange rates parallels other developments in regional co-operation for trade and other purposes, e.g. NAFTA and MERCUR. Such developments are not, however, likely to bring much closer political co-operation within each region if they are each the responsibility of a different organization (with differing membership). The architects of the UN created regional economic commissions for Europe, Asia and Latin America, but these have been solely a forum for discussion, with little or no executive responsibility. If there is to be more effective international co-operation for economic and other purposes, building more effective regional organizations must be a key part of the project.

The globalization of financial markets, and the growing vulnerability of national economies to them, make it imperative to move increasingly from national to international action to regulate and stabilize the world economy. We must update and strengthen the post-war international institutions and develop new means of international economic co-operation. Finding the will and the means to do so is one of the leading, if not *the* leading, political challenges of the new century, but one to which the New Orthodoxy has nothing to contribute.

Notes

1. *Socialism and the Condition of the People* (Labour Party, 1933).
2. *Bretton Woods, Proceedings and Documents of United Nations Monetary and Financial Conference 1944.*
3. Singh, A., '"Asian capitalism" and the financial crisis' and Grabel, I., 'Rejecting exceptionalism: reinterpreting the Asian financial crises' in *Global Instability*, Michie, J. and Grieve Smith, J. (eds.) (Routledge, 1999).
4. Chang, H-J., *The Hazard of Moral Hazard: Untangling the Asian Crisis*, World Development vol. 28, no. 4.
5. This account of the crisis and the figures quoted are based on IMF, World Bank and BIS Reports.
6. IMF *World Economic Outlook and International Capital Markets: Interim Assessment* December 1998.
7. Soros, G., *The Crisis of Global Capitalism: Open Society Endangered* (Little, Brown, 1998).
8. ul Haq, M., (ed) *The Tobin Tax: Coping with Financial Volatility* (Oxford University Press, 1996).
9. Bank of International Settlements *Survey of Foreign Exchange and Derivatives Market Activity 1998* (May 1999).
10. Luca, C., *Trading in Global Currency Markets* (Prentice Hall, 1995).
11. London Economics, *The impact of a reduction in stamp duty on UK equity transactions* (November 1999).
12. Quoted in Moggridge, D.E., *Maynard Keynes, An Economist's Biography* (Routledge, 1992).
13. Report to the US Congress of the International Financial Institution Advisory Commission (2000).

Chapter 6

A NEW ECONOMIC AGENDA

They have no vision, and when there is no vision the people perish.

Franklin D. Roosevelt

1. BREAKING THE THATCHERITE MOULD

We need a new economic agenda. It is time we put the Thatcherite consensus behind us. Adherence to it may seem the safest way for New Labour to achieve and retain power, as long as it holds sway with the majority of opinion-formers. But the fundamental assumptions underlying this consensus are at odds with the object of achieving a fairer society, which has always been the common factor in the many strands of opinion going to make up the Labour movement. Indeed much of its emphasis is also incompatible with the beliefs of One Nation Conservatism. The driving force of the Thatcherite revolution was not some abstract economic theory of monetarism, but a reaction against the very nature of a full employment society, the power it gave the unions, the egalitarian atmosphere it created and the tax burden it placed on the well-off to support universal social services. The liberal economic theories of Milton Friedman and others which were summoned up in support of the Thatcher revolution had been prevalent in right-wing circles for many years and were not in any way a response to inflationary developments in the 1970s. But these developments provided the environment in which they could flourish, not only in this country but in most of the industrialized world. The failure of post-war society to cope with the severe inflationary problems of the 1970s provided the opportunity to overturn the prevailing consensus and turn the clock back to something nearer the pre-war system. It is highly ironic that 'New' Labour should now be consolidating this reversion under the cloak of 'modernization'!

New Labour in power

In so far as Labour's traditional objective of achieving a fairer society means siding with the underdog, there is always a potential electoral majority against such a change – something which kept the Conservatives in power for 18 years. New Labour has overturned the Conservative Party's electoral majority, but not its basic political assumptions. Indeed, leading Labour ministers have gone out of their way to treat the poorest members of the community, the unemployed and others on benefit as an underclass of scroungers and second-class citizens, in a way that few Conservatives would have dared to do. This is particularly unfitting when a fundamental feature of the neo-liberal economic theories they now espouse is that there must be a large enough pool of unemployment to limit the power of the unions and avoid any danger of wage inflation – a pool which Treasury reports continually suggest is becoming too low for safety.

Gordon Brown has taken the fashionable neo-liberal prescription further than most. Not only has he put monetary policy in the hands of an independent committee of technicians at the Bank of England, but he has also (formally at any rate) renounced the use of changes in taxation or public expenditure as instruments of demand management – a dangerous abdication of power if we are faced with the threat of recession. Although as unemployment has declined, ministers have started to pay lip service to the restoration of full employment, neither their approach to policy nor their concept of how society should work is consistent with that aim.

Restoring full employment

The Government has regarded the main weapons for reducing unemployment as various 'supply-side' measures to improve skills and training and help people get jobs. Such measures are useful in themselves, but will not increase employment unless the jobs are there to fill. Achieving full employment depends on recognizing that the fundamental factor affecting the rate of unemployment is the level of demand and hence the number of jobs available. A government that has washed its hands of demand management, and whose only remit to the Bank of England is an inflation target, is hardly in a position to claim that achieving full employment is one of its major objectives. If demand management is to be geared to the achievement of full employment and not merely the avoidance of inflation, the Bank of England needs to be given a wider remit. Its objectives should be defined in terms of achieving a high and stable level of employment, and a stable and competitive exchange rate, as well as an inflation target.

Monetary policy alone cannot, however, be relied on to manage demand – particularly if we are to achieve greater exchange rate stability. Budgetary policy has an important part to play. The Chancellor's fiscal rules should be set aside, or reinterpreted, to allow more active use of the budgetary policy, particularly if recession threatens.

As the general level of unemployment falls, the problem of creating new jobs in the regions of heavy unemployment becomes increasingly important. A more active regional policy with more effective financial incentives to attract industry to the more depressed regions is an essential part of any full employment policy. The problem of regional unemployment will not necessarily be solved by devolution and encouraging each Regional Development Agency to stimulate development in its own area. This may merely mean that the stronger regions draw further ahead of the weaker ones. To improve the balance between regions, the central government must give discriminatory assistance to those with the highest levels of unemployment.

In preparation for maintaining low unemployment in a world where inflation once again becomes a major threat, the Government should establish machinery for discussing economic policy and pay issues with the TUC and CBI. Although the world economy now appears to be in greater danger of recession than renewed inflation, it would be prudent to put in place such machinery now and get it working smoothly, so that if inflationary problems re-emerge, we are in a position to tackle them without renewed resort to deflation and heavy unemployment.

2. TOWARDS A FAIRER SOCIETY

The Thatcherite revolution produced a striking increase in inequality in British society. The re-emergence of mass unemployment led to a massive redistribution of power from workers, and the unions that represent them, to employers. The effect on pay was particularly marked for those at the bottom of the income scale. Those with the least skills or qualifications were left fighting for increasingly badly-paid jobs at the bottom of the pay ladder. At the same time the desire to cut back the Welfare State meant harsher treatment for those on benefit. Meanwhile, at the other end of the scale, financial institutions began to take the lead in establishing levels of pay etc. for directors and senior managers that would formerly have been unthinkable.

Despite the fall in unemployment in the second half of the 1990s, we are still living in a grossly unequal society. The Labour Party's major aim should be to set out the road to a fairer society. Re-establishing genuine full employment is the first essential. Redefining full employment in terms of equal opportunity to compete for the available jobs dodges the issue. Levelling up the chances of getting the available jobs will not establish full employment unless there are enough jobs to go round.

Establishing a fairer society is not just a matter of redistribution through the tax and benefits system. We need to look again at the factors that establish incomes before tax. One measure which would curb excessive pay at the top would be to make it mandatory to have employee representatives on company remuneration committees which set directors' pay. At the bottom, the government's strategy should be to gradually bring up the minimum wage to a more acceptable proportion of average earnings and review it annually to maintain this relationship. An adequate level of minimum pay should obviate the need for employment credits for people without children.

Company management is being increasingly dominated by the short-term ethos of financial institutions whose immediate concern is the level of share prices rather than long-term profitability. The role and structure of companies needs to be reviewed, and company law reformed, to establish their wider responsibilities to their workforce, customers, suppliers and the community at large, as well as their shareholders. After a brief flirtation with stakeholding, the Government seems to have accepted prevailing right-wing neo-liberal views of the role of the company to an extraordinary extent. Instead of repelling EU measures to social partnership, Labour should be welcoming them. Employee representation needs to be established and strengthened at all levels of the company, including board level.

The public sector

Despite its previous criticisms, New Labour has continued the Thatcherite erosion of the public sector by privatization and the injection of private capital. The original Conservative motivation was a desire to reduce the size of the public sector; but the economic rationale was that private sector management was inherently more efficient than that in the public sector and this saving would more than compensate for the higher cost of private borrowing. The underlying fallacy, now deeply embedded in the New Orthodoxy, was that reducing government borrowing in this way 'saved public money'. On the contrary, it may mean that in the longer term the taxpayer is paying the private contractor more than they would have paid in interest if the government had borrowed the money itself. Where the use of private finance involves the chaotic fragmentation of the system, as in the railways and London Underground, the whole concept becomes absurd. We need to look at new forms of public enterprise for essential services with greater freedom from government control and the ability to borrow on their account.

Universal access to good standards of health care and education is fundamental to a fairer and more equal society. It is time to face up to the expenditure and tax implications of providing such services. The basic weakness in both the NHS and the state education system is a shortage of staff. Increasing the number of doctors, nurses and teachers is not the whole answer, but it is an essential part of it. If we are to increase the numbers employed and their pay is to increase in line with that elsewhere, public expenditure on health and education must increase as a proportion of total national income. Unless there are drastic cuts in other form of public expenditure, such as defence, this means that the proportion of national income taken in taxes must increase. It is idle to pretend that we can have it both ways: better services and lower taxes. We should be debating the fairest way to raise the increasing revenue needed, so as both to provide improved services and a more egalitarian pattern of incomes after tax. The Labour Party has made a serious mistake in committing itself to avoid any increase in the rates of income tax.

3. REBUILDING THE WELFARE STATE

The influence of the Thatcherite consensus has been especially notice-able in the area of so-called 'welfare reform', where the Government's implicit strategy has been to continue previous governments' moves away from universal benefits to increasing reliance on means-testing. This is particularly marked in the area of pensions. Their refusal to link the state pension to annual increases in earnings, rather than prices, means that it will become an increasingly inadequate substitute for lost earnings after retirement. Under the proposed Pension Credit to be introduced in 2003, half of pensioner households will be dependent on means-tested benefits to achieve a minimum standard of living. The same process of whittling away universal benefits applies to unemployment and disability benefits. A similar approach has been adopted in the case of family support, where increasing emphasis is being given to a complicated system of income-related children's benefits. If this process continues for long, universal benefits will eventually be scrapped and we shall go over to a wholly means-tested system.

Means-testing

Reliance on means-testing raises major issues of policy, which are not being fully debated. Those who receive such benefits tend to do so more as a favour from the better-off members of the community than as a return for the contributions and taxes they have paid – they are in effect treated as second-class citizens. It is no coincidence that ministers have increasingly used derogatory language about those on such benefits, with a quite disproportionate emphasis on fraud and use of phrases like 'work-shy'. This has gone along with increasing emphasis on compulsion in considering means of getting the unemployed back to work. Although the word may not be used much, the American concept of an 'underclass' has taken hold. Those involved are not regarded as fellow citizens but rather as a group apart, outside the bounds of normal society. The low uptake of means-tested benefits is a clear sign that many of those enti-tled to them fight shy of the complicated form-filling and interrogation involved, or regard them as demeaning.

The other major disadvantage of means-testing is that it discourages people on low incomes from saving, and penalizes those who do. Even under the Government's much heralded Pension Credit scheme, designed to ease the burden of the present means test, pensioners with savings incomes of between £20 and £60 a week could lose 40p in benefit for every extra £1 they receive – the same rate of 'tax' as high-income earners. This is an ironic feature of an approach ostensibly concerned to encourage as many people as possible to make their own pension arrangements. The truth is that policy-makers' overriding concern is to keep down expenditure and taxation, particularly on the better-off. Tony Blair's Middle England who make some modest provision for their old age are the main losers.

The shift towards means-testing is a retrograde movement, not an advance. There clearly remains as much need as ever for the state to provide an adequate level of pensions and other benefits – this is not something that can be left to the private sector. Future policy should be based on the principle of social insurance – that is adequate benefits received as of right, financed by a combination of social security contributions and taxation, with means-testing reduced to a minimum. The system should be made more inclusive by reviewing contribution conditions, including the lower earnings limit which creates particular difficulties for part-time women workers. The main benefits, and in particular the basic state pension, should be set at a fixed proportion of average earnings equivalent to the Minimum Income Guarantee and uprated automatically with increases in earnings.

The 'ageing time-bomb'

One of the lessons of the 1970s is that cost of benefits is highly sensitive to the proportion of the population in work. Neo-liberal economic policies, based on a low level of demand for labour and a pool of unemployment in order to avoid inflation, raise the social security bill, as we saw in the 1980s. The government should maintain a high demand for labour to facilitate higher employment rates in depressed regions and among older people. Full employment is much the best weapon for making a decent social security system affordable. The answer to the so-called 'ageing time-bomb' is not to whittle away pension provision, but to increase the number of older people, and others, at work. This requires a change in attitude among employers, and more flexible pension provision allowing people to draw their pensions over a wider age-range and acquire additional pension by retiring later. Compulsory retirement ages in both the public and private sectors should be abolished. The standard retirement age for state pensions should gradually be increased over future decades as people remain healthier and live longer.

The fact remains, however, that an adequate system of universal benefits will require higher contributions or taxes than an increasingly means-tested one. The system now being created for future generations should not be predetermined by a short-sighted election pledge not to raise income tax. The Labour Party should be offering the public a better social security system, albeit at a higher cost, together with a vigorous programme of measures to bring more people into employment who are at present excluded because of their age or where they live.

4. MAKING EUROPEAN INTEGRATION WORK

Whilst social partnership still remains an important element in the EU approach to economic and industrial policy, in other respects the New Orthodoxy is becoming increasingly dominant. The creation of EMU and the euro is the most striking symbol of this. Hitherto a currency has been widely regarded as an attribute of sovereignty under the control of the government of that area; and the formation of a European government would have been the natural precursor of adopting a common currency. But the new monetary union is being run by an independent central bank free from any form of governmental control, making it the most powerful economic institution in Europe.

For many years the economic circumstances of different countries within the monetary union may vary widely, with inflation a stronger threat in some, and unemployment more of a problem in others. A common monetary policy and level of interest rates therefore need to be supplemented by active national budgetary policies to meet their differing needs. Rather than encouraging such an essential factor in making monetary union a success, European finance ministers have

126

put themselves in an unnecessary strait-jacket by adopting the Stability and Growth Pact which strictly limits the scope for budgetary action at national level. In tune with current fashion, it has a strong deflationary bias and seriously limits the scope for running budget deficits to stimulate economies in time of recession, but it places no corresponding restriction on deflationary action. Although the Pact does indirectly acknowledge the need for fiscal action in the event of a serious recession, it effectively rules out precautionary measures to prevent it happening in the first place. Furthermore this approach fails to recognize the fact that while high interest rates may curb an inflationary boom, cuts in interest rates may be powerless to stimulate a flagging economy.

Reducing unemployment

The grip of the New Orthodoxy is apparent in the idea, strongly supported by UK ministers, that the answer to the continued high level of unemployment on the continent is more 'flexible' labour markets, which mainly means making it easier to sack people. One of the original arguments was that this would attract more foreign investment. Recent experience in the UK suggests that it also has the reverse effect of making it easier for foreign investors to withdraw when the going gets tough. One of the strengths of the social partnership approach on the continent has been the emphasis placed on stability and long-term thinking in industry, particularly important factors in the post-war success of German industry – and one which is assuming even greater importance with the development of high-technology industries which have a lead time of many years from the original research to the development of new products. It is strange that New Labour ministers are so opposed to what might have been an essential ingredient of the so-called Third Way – almost as if they were reacting against the fact that this is one reason why the British trade union movement has become so pro-European.

The key to reducing the present high level of unemployment in EMU is the adoption of more expansionary monetary and fiscal policies. In so far as the European Central Bank appears to have a strong deflationary bias and is insulated against political interference, the onus is mainly on national budgetary policies. First and foremost what is required to move in a more expansionary direction is a change in attitudes. But at the same time a renegotiation (or reinterpretation) of the Stability and Growth Pact is needed to give formal effect to such a change in emphasis. As a first step the Council of Ministers should draw up new guidelines under Article 103 of the Treaty for expansionary policies to reduce unemployment. This should provide a framework for co-ordinating national budgetary policies – here, 'co-ordination' does not mean that all member countries should be adopting the same fiscal stance (i.e. equally expansionary policies), but that the general direction is agreed and differences between countries reflect differences in their macro-economic situation.

Unless the EU tackles the unemployment problem in this way, there remains a serious danger that the social stresses caused could go beyond the present occasional outbreaks of violence and xenophobia and lead to a major resurgence of support for right-wing extremism. While the Union has successfully ruled out forever the possibility of another Franco-German War – one of the greatest triumphs of post-war statesmanship – there is still a possibility that democracy somewhere in Europe could be threatened by disillusionment with the present political leadership.

Tax harmonization

As economic integration continues, the question of tax harmonization will come increasingly to the fore. It is clear that within a common market there are limits to the extent to which sales taxes can vary between states – and the difference in the rates of tax on alcoholic drinks between the two sides of the English Channel clearly exceeds this. But increasing mobility is not confined to goods; it applies to an even greater extent to financial transactions of various kinds. Effective taxation in this field will depend increasingly on European, and indeed global, co-operation and harmonization of tax regimes. The British government should resist the pressure of City interests and co-operate more closely with their European colleagues in this field.

Future structure

The coming enlargement of the Union will reinforce the need to take decisions on its future structure. Initially it can continue with a modified version of the present system with amended voting weights and a new formula for appointing Commissioners. But in the longer run more fundamental decisions are needed as to what functions should be undertaken on a European, rather than national, basis, and what is the most effective democratic constitution for European government. The basic choice, which must be faced sooner or later, is whether to continue indefinitely on what is essentially an international basis, albeit with European institutions and a European Parliament, or to move towards some form of elected European Government. The latter might involve the direct election of a President, and possibly members of his Cabinet, or a parliamentary system with the Government drawn directly from MEPs. In either case the principle would be that the European Government would only have limited specified powers and all other powers would rest with national governments. It seems reasonable to assume that the greater the powers to be exercised on a European, rather than national basis, the more likely it is that a federal solution will ultimately be adopted.

The fact that 'federalism' has became a dirty word (particularly on the right) is not just a simple matter of nationalism: it is also part and parcel of the neo-liberal antagonism to any government interference with the economic system and the sanctity of markets. 'Government is dangerous enough at national level, don't let's make it any worse by introducing any further levels of government,' is their implicit outcry. But at a time when finance and industry are increasingly operating on a regional or global scale, the responsibilities which used to fall solely on a national government must increasingly involve governance on a wider scale.

EMU: to join or not to join?

The immediate question dominating the UK's relations with the EU is whether, or when, we should join EMU. This raises very difficult issues, but the one thing that should be clear is that it would be disastrous to join unless we do so at a competitive exchange rate. To join when the pound was overvalued in relation to the euro would seal the fate of many more British manufacturing firms. By the time, after a painful period of readjustment, our costs were eventually in line with those on the continent, much of our capacity in industries, like steel and motors, would have gone for good. A fundamental condition for joining at all should be that the exchange rate is right – that means more like 2.40 DM to 2.60 DM, or 1.2 to 1.3 euro to the pound. The key issues involved are:-

1. How deeply do we want to get involved in further European political and economic integration?
2. How acceptable is the EMU regime with an independent European central bank?
3. What would be the economic consequences for the UK of adopting a common currency and interest rates?

All these considerations must be taken into account.

The first question is the most difficult, because we have strong political and cultural ties with the rest of the English-speaking world, the Commonwealth and the US, but we also are economically a part of Europe. Much therefore depends on whether the European system is one whose values and political constitution we are happy to take on board. On this basis we might expect the EMU set-up to be more acceptable to neo-liberals than the rest of us, though it is doubtful if that is the case. For my own part, I do not believe we should enter EMU as at present constituted. To do so, would reduce the chances of our achieving and maintaining full employment.

It is misleading, moreover, to suggest that there is simply a stark choice as to whether to join EMU or continue with the present free-floating regime for sterling. There is a strong case for an intermediate solution of managing the rate of the pound (and other EU currencies outside EMU) to the euro. This would require a new ERM-style agreement – one which must be carefully designed to avoid the pitfalls of the past. The essential changes are:-

1. Parities should be adjusted in small and relatively frequent steps, rather than waiting for large adjustments in crisis conditions. This would radically reduce the scope for speculative gains.

2. Market intervention to keep rates within their stated bands should be automatic, rather than dependent on *ad hoc* arrangements between central banks. A stabilization fund should be set up for this purpose.

An arrangement of this type in Europe could pave the way for parallel arrangements to stabilize exchange rates both regionally and on a global scale. But again, we should only enter at a competitive rate for sterling.

5. TAMING GLOBAL FINANCE

The instability of the global financial system is a threat to economic growth and employment, not just in developing countries but throughout the world. Financial markets are in danger of becoming the master, rather than the servant, of industry and the real economy. Evolving more powerful and effective machinery for international economic co-operation must be a major political objective in the coming decade. The British government is in a good position to give a lead, with London a major international financial centre, and our close links with the United States as well as our membership of the European Union.

Damping down speculation

There are three closely interlinked aspects of this instability, as evidenced in the Asian crisis: the volatility of international capital flows, bubbles in stock market prices, and exchange rate instability. In a typical crisis, inflows of foreign capital and booms in share prices feed on each other and put upward pressure on exchange rates. Then a sudden reversal of sentiment leads to an outflow of capital, a stock market collapse and a fall in exchange rates. Measures are needed to tackle these inter-related phenomena on a wide front.

The premature liberalization of capital controls played a major part in the Asian crisis. The IMF should no longer seek to ban the use of capital controls by developing countries either as a precautionary or crisis measure. The industrialized countries should consider means of ensuring a

131

greater, and more stable, flow of long-term capital to developing countries, including a more active role for the World Bank.

Any movement to reform has so far been mainly concentrated on improving the prudential regulation of financial institutions. Finance ministers of the leading industrial countries have set up the Financial Stability Forum to co-ordinate the activities of supervising authorities. The Basel Committee on Banking Supervision has put forward proposals for revising capital backing requirements: for example, to remove the incentive to banks to make short-term, rather than longer-term, loans.

But the fundamental problem of excessive leverage in the financial system has yet to be fully recognized. The ability to take a large chance of gain (or risk of loss) for a small stake lies behind virtually all speculative movements. The extent of such risk-taking depends on the availability of credit (directly or indirectly) for such purposes, and the evolution of derivative instruments which have increased the ability of participants to bet on stock market prices, interest rates or exchange rates for a payment of only a fraction of the gross sums involved. More emphasis is needed on restraining forms of bank lending which may fuel financial speculation; and stock market and other regulators should look more closely at the types of derivatives available.

Taxation of financial market transactions could be a useful means of damping down speculative activity. The long-standing proposal, now supported by George Soros, to impose a small (Tobin) tax of, say, 0.1 per cent on all foreign exchange transactions would both serve this purpose and raise funds for international purposes such as development aid, environmental projects and peace-keeping. But in addition, the issue of wider taxation of financial transactions must now come onto the political agenda. The UK and other countries already levy taxes on stock market transactions, but with the development of global markets these need to be harmonized and extended. Otherwise in the longer run market activity will gravitate to the areas with the lowest or no taxes, and 'tax competition' will whittle away taxes on large corporations and rich investors at the expense of the ordinary taxpayer.

Managing exchange rates

Exchange rates lie at the heart of the international financial system, and a more stable exchange rate regime is the least discussed, but most fundamental, reform that we should be addressing. Both fixed and freely floating exchange rates have serious disadvantages: 'fixed' rates tend to be adjusted only under crisis conditions; floating rates leave industry at the mercy of inappropriate and unforeseeable movements in rates. We need to devise systems of managed, but flexible, rates which can be adjusted to changing conditions, (such as relative movements in costs) but which provide greater stability. The general model for such systems should be to have publicly stated parities and bands (as proposed above for members and non-members of EMU) with rates reviewed, say, monthly; any necessary changes made in small steps; and automatic intervention through special stabilization funds set up for this purpose (rather than by central banks).

Moving towards a more stable, managed exchange rate regime requires a two-tier approach, with (a) regional systems (which may vary between different regions), and (b) global arrangements to link the rates between them. Initially this would embody a European grouping, managing the rates between the euro and non-EMU countries in the EU; a North and Latin American group based on the dollar; and an Asian group based initially on the yen. Such a tripolar system would then require a global arrangement (under the IMF) to manage the rates between these three groupings. But until such groupings were established, informal moves to manage the relation between the three major currencies would help to achieve greater stability.

An inevitable corollary of a more stable system of managed exchange rates would be that countries would need to keep their interest rates broadly in line – subject to differences in their inflation rates. This would mean that budgetary rather than monetary policy would have to be acknowledged as the main instrument of national demand management.

Reforming international institutions

A new and more stable international financial system will require changes in both the policies and structures of the present international financial institutions. In particular, the IMF should stop prescribing deflationary measures which increase the risk of massive increases in unemployment in countries in difficulties, and instead help them to stabilize their economies in such a way as to maintain employment. The Fund should also recognize the democratic right of member countries to determine their own economic structure and not dictate highly political changes, like privatization. The voting structures of both the IMF and the World Bank should be updated to give the developing countries more weight.

The structure of the present multitude of international organizations, the IMF and World Bank, the UN institutions and the OECD needs to be streamlined and updated. Regional organizations should play a greater part in any new structure and developing countries should have a more powerful voice. Given the large number of countries (around 200) which now make up the membership of international institutions, more effective international governance in future may depend on a two-tier system of representation and decision-making, with regional organizations eventually becoming part of the formal constitution of global organizations such as the IMF and World Bank. The ultimate objective must be to establish a comprehensive new structure of world governance incorporating the IMF and World Bank into a new United Nations with a democratic dimension.

6. A BETTER WAY

If our elected governments are to control our own economic destiny, and we are not to be at the mercy of the vagaries of financial markets, governments must work closely together to establish more effective means of world economic governance. There is no excuse for politicians wringing their hands helplessly and pleading that they are powerless in the face of globalization of markets. Given the will of governments to act together, it is perfectly possible for them to reassert control over economic policy, and make the greater interdependence of national economies a force for progress rather than a threat of disaster. The idea that, as national economies become more closely interlinked, governments should stand back and leave industry to the mercy of global financial markets is a retrogression to the dominant beliefs of the inter-war period, which exacted a disastrous economic and political price.

The New Orthodoxy, with its neo-liberal economic foundations, is three-quarters of a century out of date. It has no effective answers to today's problems of achieving greater stability in a globalized international economy. It is fundamentally opposed to the concepts of full employ-ment and a more equal society. Powerful as this consensus may still be, it is not one which social democratic parties should embrace, as it is hostile to all they stand for. So too is the accompanying predominance of finance over industry, with the short-term outlook and instability inherent in financial markets. There is another way: the road to equal citizenship, based on co-operation between government, unions and employers to maintain full employment and establish a fairer society, and the willing-ness of national governments to pool their sovereignty in order to develop more effective international institutions and achieve greater global economic stability. This is the challenge of the new century.

POSTSCRIPT

If there were any doubts that the next Blair government was set to continue consolidating the Thatcher revolution, the election campaign should have dispelled them. On what became the key election issue of improving health, education and other public services, Labour's failure to acknowledge the need to raise additional tax revenue if there are to be any substantial improvements in these services contrasted strongly with the Liberal Democrats' more forthright stance on this issue. Labour's commitment not to increase the basic or top rates of income tax, and to extend the 10p tax band, now leave it with little room to manoeuvre.

While Tony Blair's attitude to Europe has been less antagonistic than William Hague's, he has continued his attack on the continental style of social partnership under the banner of 'modernization' and 'reform'. In particular he fought to the last ditch against the EU proposals to improve employees' rights to consultation. Again, Gordon Brown's opposition to tax harmonization may safeguard the interests of the City and the rich investor, but is in danger of leaving the ordinary taxpayer shouldering an increasing part of the tax burden. In defending Labour's tax commitments, Tony Blair made it plain that in an era of tax competition between countries, he saw no point in raising taxes on high earners or business. The idea of using taxation as a means of redistribution (at least openly, if not by stealth) is no longer on New Labour's agenda.

Labour's proposals to make more use of private companies in the NHS and local education implicitly reflect a Thatcherite belief that private sector management is always the best, and a lack of concern to preserve and enhance the public service ethos which has been a traditional feature of the teaching and caring professions. It is significant that these proposals were effectively smuggled into the manifesto at the last minute without prior public discussion. In view of the widespread concern of many Labour supporters and those who work in the public sector, the object was presumably to be able to claim that there is now an electoral mandate for them and that the new government must push ahead as rapidly as possible without further debate.

It is no wonder *The Economist* supported Tony Blair as 'the only credible conservative currently available'; and *The Times*, for the first time in its history, exhorted its readers to support Labour, as the party best fitted to the task of 'consolidating the core aspects of Thatcherism and extending them to fresh areas of policy'. It is a tragic irony that Labour's first clear mandate for a second term in office should have been achieved by stealing its opponents' clothes.

INDEX

138